Papken Injarabian

AZO THE SLAVE BOY
AND HIS ROAD TO FREEDOM

translated from Armenian by

Elisabeth Eaker

Gomidas Institute
London

ISBN 978-1-909382-16-9

Gomidas Institute
42 Blythe Rd.
London W14 0HA
United Kingdom
www.gomidas.org
info@gomidas.org

*This work is dedicated to the victims
of the Armenian Genocide of 1915*

ACKNOWLEDGMENTS

The translator wishes to express her most sincere gratitude to Linda Parseghian, her cousin and Papken's niece, for her indispensable assistance with correcting and proofreading, her professional advice, and continuous support throughout this family endeavor.

Special thanks also go to the translator's husband, Lawrence H. Eaker, Jr., for his constructive criticism and participation in the overall correction of this translation.

Finally, I thank the Gomidas Institute, and in particular its founding director, Ara Sarafian, for their interest in this historical document and ultimate publication.

> I know the Lord is always with me.
> I will not be shaken, for he is right beside me....
> (He) will show me the way of life.

> Psalm 16: 8-11

INTRODUCTION

Papken Injarabian, my father, was born in 1906 in Amasia, Turkey. He was the youngest of five children and was growing up in a loving Armenian family. When Ottoman Turkey entered World War I, his older brothers were conscripted but the family never saw them again. The Turkish government then ordered the evacuation of Amasia and neighboring villages, as part of the planned deportation and destruction of Ottoman Armenians. On June 21, 1915, nine-year old Papken, his parents and two sisters had to leave behind their beloved home. They were forced to march for hundreds of miles across the treacherous mountains. The heat was intense and they lacked food and water. People died by the thousands from starvation, dehydration, and exhaustion. Along the way, they saw piles of corpses, evidence of the mass executions of their fellow countrymen by the Turks. During the exodus, young Papken experienced many losses. One of his sisters was given away to Kurds, and his father was murdered. Later, another Kurd separated Papken and the rest of his family from the convoy, threatened to kill them, and abducted his remaining sister. Soon after, his frail mother died from cholera and overwhelming sorrow. Suddenly, Papken was alone in the world. He was now an orphan and was taken in by Kurds as a slave. In order to stay alive, he had no choice but to become a Muslim, and was renamed Azo. During his enslavement, which lasted more than four years, he ran away many times and had nine masters. He had to endure the cruelty of his masters and their families, starvation, and despair. He never bathed and never slept on a mattress. One day, he heard about an orphanage in Urfa, which rescued many young Armenians like him. This news gave him hope and he was determined to make his way to Urfa. His memoir is a story of survival and how he found the strength to overcome fear, suffering and hardship, thanks to his perseverance and profound faith in God.

Elisabeth Eaker
Paris, 4 December 2014

AZO THE SLAVE BOY
AND HIS ROAD TO FREEDOM

I

My name is Papken Injarabian. In exile, as I will explain shortly, I was called Azo, the name given to me by my Kurdish abductors. I was born in Amasia, a town in Asia Minor, located near the southern part of the Black Sea. I was barely nine years old when the exodus began in June of 1915. Because I was so young, I was allowed to leave with my family and was not separated from them, as were many other children.

This narrative begins at the time when my two brothers, Hampartsoum and Hagop, were enlisted in the Turkish army. I attended school and was growing up in the warmth of my home, surrounded by my loving parents and two older sisters. One day after school, I found my eldest brother at home as he was sick. I had not seen him in years. Why was he back? Was he on leave? Had he deserted? It was a mystery to me. My mother was taking care of him but I wondered why she seemed so upset.

Some weeks later, the Turkish government issued orders for our school to be closed. Hampartsoum recovered and left home again. The following day, my mother gave me a package and said, "Take this to your brother, who is at the school." I took the package to my dear school and discovered my brother locked in the principal's office. (This was the very office where I had been sent when caught playing hookie recently; my punishment was to kneel for several hours.) The school was taken over by soldiers and I don't remember how long this occupation lasted. Once my brother had departed with the others, the school reopened and we students were allowed to return. I used to hear my father discuss the events with concern. Finally, one day, the school closed again, never to reopen. At that point, the situation took a real tragic turn. One morning on the way to work, all the Armenian men were rounded up by police officers, backed by reinforcements. These men were sent to jail. When the women saw this, they attempted to bring food to their husbands and sons but the police forced them to leave. The streets were empty and whoever ventured outside risked going to jail or being beaten, sometimes to death.

Our nearest neighbor, Marouk Agha, manufactured silk in his home, part of which had been turned into a factory. He was taken away with his five children in spite of his advanced age and social status. Tortured, he was ordered to reveal where he had hidden weapons and munitions. After being subjected to extreme pain, he finally confessed that his eldest son knew the location of the secret hiding place. His son, in turn, became the executioner's victim. Exhausted, he admitted that a few weapons were buried under a tree. After his confession, he was beaten some more, his nails were pulled off and he died from his wounds. His name was Minas and thousands of his compatriots died under similar conditions. Others, with their hands tied up behind them, were taken to the Devrendi Valley and slaughtered. Their remains were thrown in a pile. Ghabash Ali, a man from the village of Vermish, was a volunteer serving the regime. His job was to gather and list the victims' possessions, including jewels pulled off their bodies.

Never will I forget the names of the individuals responsible for the massacres, deportations, and executions. Although a complete list would be too long to cite, they include: Centener Yous Bashi Nouri, Topji Oghlou Shoukri, Gendarma Guomandani, Condraji, Tin Tin Assan, Muhendis Resmy, Tushji Hatez, Temerkhanedji Molla Bekir and his brother Kalil, and many more. Of course, I learned this by listening to the women and old men's conversations. Still, I could see for myself the extreme distress of my people and the women lamenting between their tears.

On June 21, 1915, we were ordered to be exiled. Policemen escorted us onto the road of exile, and we slowly left our homes behind. The government gave each family a cart, pulled by two oxen or horses. This way, everyone could carry away some of their belongings. Along the way, we encountered other groups like ours. After walking for several days, we arrived in Shar Kishla, a small town where we found a large crowd of our brothers coming from all directions. Many of us began suffering from hunger. My father, who was a butcher, bought sheep from the Kurds, slaughtered them, and sold the pieces of meat, so that we would all have something to eat.

Several days later, the Turks from Shar Kishla began to gather all of the boys and girls, including my two sisters and me. Other families were deprived of their children in the same manner. The Turks packed us in a large house and sent messengers all around announcing that Armenian children were available to anyone wanting to take them. The peasants, thus alerted, came along and chose children the way they would have chosen cattle. My sisters, Margaret (Markarid) and Mariam, begged our guardians to allow me to be free, considering my young age. They succeeded in their laments. I ran to my father and mother and found them in tears at my arrival. Margaret and Mariam were separated and given away, as they had to submit to the common fate.

I resumed the exodus with my parents. As soon as we left Shar Kishla, our tormentors – Kurds, Turks, Zazas, and Circassians – struck and plundered, leaving masses of dead and wounded bodies on the road, adding to those who had already perished from exhaustion and hunger. Our attackers were hungry as wolves and with hatchets, sticks, stones –or even without any weapons – rushed through the hordes of exiles in an effort to exterminate us.

My father, whose life had been spared up to that point, grabbed my hand and tried to escape with me. But a Kurd came

Amasia, the ancestral home of the Injarabian family.

up right behind us and caught him by the throat. He yelled, "*Para! Para!*" (Money! Money!) while raising a hatchet in the air with his other hand. He struck my father's head with the back of the hatchet, causing him to bleed. Suddenly, the aggressor released my father and fled. Four other Kurds were dragging a howling old man down an abyss. We then returned to our miserable flock, abandoning all hope.

Later, we encountered two cars arriving from the other direction. The occupants, military men carrying weapons, quickly got out and started firing in all directions to scatter our aggressors who panicked and receded. We took advantage of the situation to reassemble and the group resumed its path. A rumor spread that we had been spared for the moment, thanks to a few Turkish and German officers who may have been moved by witnessing such misery. We stopped to spend the night and my mother prepared our meager dinner of herbs and grass we had picked along the way. She made it in a copper pot, the only cooking equipment we had left. A Kurd appeared and demanded to have the copper pot, which appealed to him because of its fine shape and quality. When my father flatly refused, the Kurd retorted hatefully, "I will have it!" and was gone.

II

The day after this incident, the Kurd was waiting for our group to pass by, holding a gun in his hand. Pulling my father towards him, he took him aside and threatened to kill him. My mother and I were crying and begging for mercy. We knelt in front of the villain promising all our possessions in exchange for my father's life. We brought him our measly belongings, including the copper pot – the very object of his desire – and he carried away whatever pleased his heart. The sacrifice of our remaining wealth had allowed my father to live a few days longer.

As we proceeded with the march, our convoy passed through Hasanchelebi and Hekimhan, near Malatia and Ghrukh Geoze. We had been away from our home for two months. At Ferenjelar, all the families were definitively separated and the surviving men captured – their hands tied behind them. The last time I saw my father, he was standing next to his best friend, Heokelek. My mother was crying and I can still hear his last words before parting, "That's enough, they can kill me now, even skin me alive if they want!" All the men disappeared and suddenly, that was it. Without a doubt, they had been executed! There I was, all alone with my mother, without any food or money.

When a new raid was announced, a woman from our village begged my mother to let her tie a belt containing gold coins around my body, underneath my clothes. Since I was young, I wouldn't attract any attention. I wore the belt and she also entrusted me with a kind of ball made of cloth and strings which held some change. I was supposed to carry it around innocently, as if it were a toy. Everybody was searched and plundered, but as expected, I was spared. My mother, who only had two *kurush*, decided we would tell the woman that the ball had been confiscated. When she came back, we returned the belt with the gold coins but I told her what we had agreed upon. She was very angry, but our extreme destitution left no room for any remorse. My mother was very thrifty with the money. She bought a blanket for eight *kurush* from other exiles to protect us from the cold at night. We had hardly used it, when after three nights, it was stolen by Kurds. They pulled it off us while we slept. We complained to the police but they made no effort to help us.

We walked on with our neighbors trying not to be separated from one another. Among them were Bulbul Hanem, Marouk Artur's wife, Minas's son's wife, Mrs. Aghavni Merdinian with her daughter Siranoush, and her son Haroutioun, who was ten. My mother watched me closely fearing she would lose me. She carried me on her back when danger arose or when I was too tired. She used to say, "I don't think of myself – I can only think of you."

Sometimes we stopped in places where no water could be found. I still have a vivid image in my mind of a woman on the ground, panting – dying of thirst and exhaustion, only able to utter one sound: "wa ... wa ... wa ..." Others, having discovered a mud puddle, were drinking from it or wetting a cloth to moisten their lips. Wherever our caravan stopped, there was evidence that others had been there before us: corpses left on the premises and little children abandoned and crying. I recall seeing toddlers, left in a hole, looking at us, their eyes begging to come with us. They were too young to speak but could not understand why we left without bringing them along. As she passed by this hole to fetch some water, Siranoush's mother said, "Siranoush, since your child died, take one of these children and make him yours. Time will go by and if your husband returns, you will present this child as your own." She carried away the smallest one who was lying naked on the ground. The other starving children believed we were also going to pick them up, too. Alas, the child didn't survive. He died the next day in Siranoush's arms. It was impossible to count how many orphans were likewise abandoned and sentenced to such a horrible death.

III

We continued to march forward. My mother guided my steps in order to avoid any contact with the dead bodies that were scattered along the ground. Up to now, Mrs. Merdinian was lucky to still have a donkey, which carried both of our families' worn out clothes. Her son Aroutioun was perched on it, when a Kurd with a large knife appeared. He threw the child on the ground, leaving with the donkey, which had been so useful to all of us. The police did nothing to help us get the animal back. A piece of bread was even stolen from my hand as I was bringing it to my mouth. It was the exile stealing from the exile, the poor harming those as poor as himself. Thus, we would secretly eat the smallest morsel, only after making sure we were completely alone and out of sight.

It was during this period that the young Turks and Kurds were dashing into the crowd to forcibly seize and carry away girls and young women. They killed a mother who was protecting her daughter and if they met any resistance, they would grab the girl by her hair and drag her along on the ground.

We finally reached a river, which spared us briefly, allowing us to drink, wash ourselves and our clothes. It was also an opportunity for some of the exiles to jump in the water to end their lives. At the sight of the water, a woman rushed towards it in a fury and threw herself in the river. She was walking in the water with no fear until she disappeared. We could see her long hair floating on the surface. But the river didn't want her and pushed her aside towards what seemed to be a little island in the middle. In fact, it was a mound of corpses and I wondered how the current had managed to gather them at this very place. She was thus thrust against the dead bodies and we could see her weep and fight and struggle at their approach. It was as if they were saying, "Since no one has come to mourn us, cry woman until your tears dry out." At last, she set herself free and returned to the current, where she disappeared. She had paid a dreadful tribute of love and brotherhood to all those forgotten and left unburied. Many women chose to die the same way, after ending their children's lives. Having witnessed all this, we continued on.

At this point, we were climbing up a very steep mountain. It was extremely hot and the odor of death was unbearable. We couldn't continue without protecting our noses and mouths with a rag tied around our faces. As overwhelmed and exasperated as we were, we scarcely wondered what our coming fate would be. My mother carried me, but I realized she was tired, so I got back on my feet. I stayed very close to her because there was the danger of lost children being slaughtered. She was protecting and guiding me between pieces of sharp broken bones and swollen dead bodies, that were rotting under the sun. As we approached the top of the mountain, the pass was so narrow we could only proceed one by one. At the bottom was a ravine; on top, more climbing with no hope in sight. What made it even more treacherous was the inability to see anything in the pitch, black night. Fortunately, we began to descend, which was somewhat of a relief. However, our walk down the mountain seemed to go on for an endless number of hours.

We whispered amongst ourselves that the next destination would be that of our extermination. Our group included no more men, only women and children. I don't know how many of us were left, but our line of exiles had thinned out dramatically, due to the losses that had occurred along the way. Those at the front of the convoy, which was led by police officers, started out by keeping up with the pace of the horses, but gradually slowed down. My mother and I usually stood in the middle of the group, but were further delayed by the paltry meal of grass and herbs we had prepared and were eating. Now, stripped of practically everything, we wrapped together our few remaining belongings, threw them on our shoulders in a bundle, and used it as a pillow at night. We often put the bundles together with our friends, as a kind of makeshift, uncomfortable mattress upon which to lay down the children.

Finally, we reached the bottom of the mountain. When night fell, we stopped, pressed against one another, exhausted and tortured by hunger and thirst. Fumbling, we searched for a place to rest our heads: a mound, a stone, our bundle, or a bit of wreckage left by Providence or anything else. Upon awakening, we greeted one another and asked how well everyone had slept after such a long and painful journey. In the morning light, one person was shocked to discover that in his haste and fatigue, he had been sleeping on a human torso: a dead man's body!

At daybreak, we began to stir and the birds themselves were starting to come to life and sing. We didn't know where we were. Not far from our group, we noticed a lifeless body on the ground, partially covered with an old cloth and a five or six-year-old child seated next to it. Swarms of buzzing flies, fat and small, green and black, were circling the body. They would get under the cloth as if going to a feast, come out staggering but not yet full, and return while the child tried to shoo them off in a slow and mechanical motion. How long had the child been repeating this movement? No one could tell. But he did it with exemplary courage and looked worn out by it. Some of us approached him and an older woman asked softly, "My boy, what are you doing?" In a barely perceptible voice, he answered, "My mother asked me to stay close by her until she can get up and give me some water and bread." A woman lifted up the rag covering the body, which served as a shroud as well, and we could all see a wide open belly crawling with worms. Turk or Kurd, what human being barbarous enough could so savagely have plunged a knife into the bowels of this poor woman? Who knows what had happened? The child, starving and naked, was faithfully watching over his mother. We searched for bread and brought him some but he looked startled at those who fed him, not understanding why his mother was not giving him the bread. However, he slowly started nibbling on it.

Some who had ventured a little further, told us they had discovered a rice mill towards which the river's current carried bodies of nude girls and young women. Had they ended their lives to escape their executioners or had they been killed? The river kept its secret. The name of this place was Kürtler Kaymakamlik. Those horrid sights prevented us from attempting suicide if the idea had ever crossed our minds. Horrified, we left the village, taking the faithful orphan with us.

In front of us stood yet another huge mountain we had to climb. Its terrifying name struck fear into all of us. In Turkish, it was called "*Nal gheran palan deoken, ghoush ouchmaz kevran yetishmez daghe,*" a description which included numerous warnings. In English, it meant: "The mountain that breaks the horses' shoes, that tears apart their saddles, that is inaccessible to birds, and that caravans cannot cross."

The lost child found near his mother's body, who we had taken with us, died, overcome by fatigue before reaching the summit of this sinister mountain. Another death!

IV

And we continued our tribulations.

The unbearable heat made me terribly thirsty. My mother comforted me and tried to cheer me up by saying, "A little more patience, my son, we'll soon find water." This hope of promised water lasted until evening. Finally, we arrived at a valley where our caravan could make a stop near a small river. As soon as I saw the water, I ran and drank it without restraint. When I got up from drinking, my head spun around and I collapsed onto my mother's lap. When I felt better, I got up again, still with a strong urge to drink more water. This time my mother came with me and we discovered corpses in the same water I had drunk so plentifully! We could see the current gliding along these floating bodies, moving them softly in an illusion of life.

How many times did this happen to us? How many times did we drink the polluted water from rivers? We walked upstream in search of clear water but there were more dead – more bodies that seemed to be awaiting our arrival. Thus, my mother discouraged me from going further. "If you continue walking my son, someone could show up and kill us. The further you go, the more bodies you'll come across. You can drink here, the deaths won't hurt you. See how clear and pure this running water is!"

When I reflect back on my country's water, I remember how pure and resistant to impurities it was, since even corpses could not spoil it. In any case, we had to content ourselves with it, since neither rivers, nor still or running waters were free of rotting bodies. The following day, we set out again. It was still very hot, but the sight of the river and contact with water had somewhat refreshed and restored us. We were even able to speed up our pace to reach the evening campsite in less time. The length between two stops varied and some days, we would walk much further than others.

Suddenly, the Euphrates appeared in front of us. It was a wonderful sight to behold: the large, still river was shining like a star all the way to the horizon and we were filled with joy at the thought of so much water being offered to us. The river marked the end of our day's march, and we stopped along its banks. We went into the water to quench our thirst. Despite our misery, we were a dignified and clean people, and felt relieved to wash our bodies and rags. But here again on the river, we could see corpses drifting away: sometimes solitary, sometimes gathered. The current carried them to the sea and they seemed to flow to a meeting place they could not avoid – a place where they were all expected.

A young lad who was bathing near us was swept away by the water, and we saw him struggle until he reached the opposite bank of the river. After desperate efforts, he emerged from the water alive and probably thought he was safe. But a dozen Kurds arrived, used him as a target, and took turns shooting at him while they laughed. He was yelling and begging, he stumbled and got back up several times, but his executioners pursued him relentlessly until he finally fell, lifeless. These cruel men had no pity for a poor lad the great river had spared. They were worse than wild animals and boasted of their crime as a glorious deed. They had to sacrifice another innocent victim, as if all the dead already surrounding them had not satisfied their appetite. Perhaps Death may have been waiting for the young man that day, since all the courage he displayed did not change the course of his fate. From the other bank, I could see the small boisterous group of murderers walking away and still laughing about their exploit.

We stayed on the banks of the Euphrates for two days. Being in such close proximity to this beautiful river and its green shores brought some happiness to our hearts. An order was issued to break up the camp so we left that spot and the Euphrates disappeared from our view. There were no more mountains to cross for the moment. It was as if we had ascended and reached our *Golgotha*, the highest point of our suffering. Now we were proceeding across a plain.

My mother made me a pair of clumsy shoes to wear out of rags she collected from all the heaps of dead bodies. She didn't want me to walk barefoot. She and her companions were doing the same, and trying their best to stay close together to avoid separating.

After a few days, we again arrived at the Euphrates and with it, the assurance that we would not die of thirst. However, instead of flowing along, it stood in front of us as a barrier, which prevented us from moving further. We stopped to camp and this time everyone was seized by fear because it was impossible to cross this wide stretch of water. We wondered if the time had now come for us to be slaughtered and turned into a burial ground! A deep sadness had come over us. After spending a night, then a day, then another night in this state of uncertainty, some boats finally arrived in the morning. One by one, we climbed inside until all of us were transferred from one bank to the other. This took place over a two-day period. The boarding was difficult and to reach the small crafts we had to enter the water up to our waists, encumbered by children and packages. One poor woman who didn't climb inside the boat quickly enough hung to its side desperately. A short way off, the Kurdish scullers steering the boat used their oars to hit her on her hands and head so brutally that she was forced to let go. In spite of her struggling, she was rushed into the waters right beneath our eyes! It appeared that even such a trivial situation as arriving late to the boat could lead to a dreadful end. Others suffered a similar fate, perishing along the way, so that when the boats finally made the crossing, the river received a new supply of victims.

Here was how a crossing took place: As soon as we climbed into the boat, we were all gathered at its center and submitted to a meticulous search for money, sparing no parts of our bodies or folds of our clothes. Anticipating this looting, some women swallowed their belongings and several died in indescribable sufferings, which had become a common practice from the beginning of our exodus.

Finally, we reached the other side of the water. We were forced to abandon our bundles in the boats and they were piled up by the river bank out of our reach. There we stood on the wet sand, soaked and deprived of everything for two days. Some women went over to the police officers and begged them to let the exiles recover a few belongings, which were of no particular interest to them. After first stealing the best items, the police yielded to the women's request.

As we continued on our path away from the river, we encountered groups of Kurds who were plundering corpses, many of whom had died of disease. These Kurds were in search of valuables and ripped jewelry off the bodies, unburied the dead to undress them in search of hidden money, and even wore their clothes!

Passing through abandoned villages, we stealthily grabbed food and other objects from open houses, churches and fields – anything that might help us survive.

V

News was circulating from one convoy to another. This is how, one morning, we learned that my sister Margaret, who was 18 and had been separated from us at Shar Kishla – had fled and joined the caravan behind us. In fact, some days later, before we left the campsite, the convoy behind caught up with us and I rejoiced in seeing her. She had been looking for us. The emotions and happiness we felt from our reunion were boundless! From now on, the three of us would face these terrible ordeals together.

A few days later, we set out again. We had hardly enjoyed being reunited, when my mother became sick and could not walk anymore. She said, "Since I cannot follow you, let me die here and the two of you keep on going. You are young and you might have a chance to survive." This made us feel utterly desperate. Not only was our mother seriously ill, but we had no food or money left. Some Kurds were escorting the caravan with provisions and a few donkeys to ride. They sold bread, water, and sometimes fruit to the exiles. The donkeys could be rented for a short period of time, for people who were too exhausted to walk. Although we were extremely needy, we could not afford anything. Confronted with this situation, our mother came up with an idea which she thought could be a way to save our lives. She shared her idea with my sister, who agreed. At that very moment, a middle-aged Kurd went by on his donkey. My mother stopped him and said, "I'll give you my daughter if you take us with you."

The Kurd looked at my sister closely, and seemed to appreciate the offer, because according to the rules and customs of his country, a woman was worth a lot of money.

With smiles and what we took for compliments, he accepted the deal. My mother was then pulled up on the donkey and I sat behind her. He discreetly turned us away from the convoy, thus escaping the police's vigilance. Along the way, he stopped and brought us some fresh water, which we drank to our satisfaction. We recovered some strength. Here we were – the four of us – proceeding on our journey: My mother and I on the donkey, he and Margaret on foot, following each other, without a word. After some time, my mother asked him when we would reach his home. He told us, "In only an hour." One to two hours went by. My mother asked again, "Is it still far away?" "No, you'll be there in half an hour." Three or four hours had passed since we were separated from our group of brothers, and we were still walking.

Suddenly, we arrived at the entrance of a small village by the name of Aghmughara (Akmagara, the village of caves). While passing through, we met two Armenian women, who were

(Below, left to right). My older brother, Hampartsoum, who went to the army before the deportations. Next to him is my sister Mariam, who remained behind in Shar Kishla. In the middle is my father, Avedis, who was with us during deportations, until Ferenjelar. Next to him, sitting, is my sister Margaret (Markarid), who was abducted by a Kurd. Next to her is me, Papken, who wrote these lines. These images come from different places and were mounted together. Unfortunately, I could not find any images of my mother or my brother, Hagop.

[Image and caption from Papken's original published memoir in Armenian.]

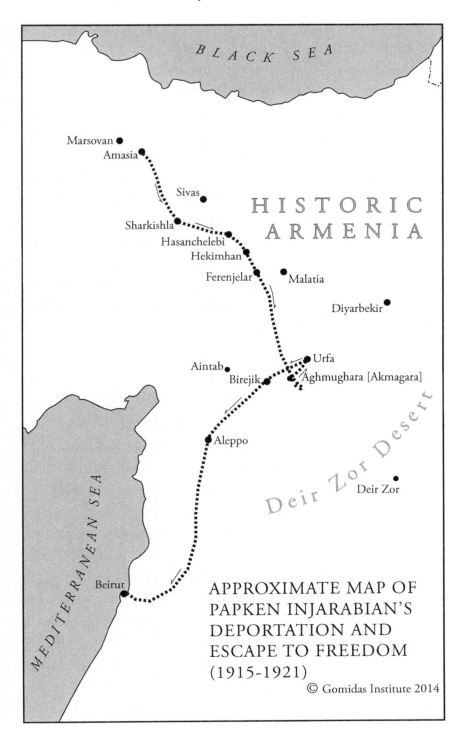

APPROXIMATE MAP OF
PAPKEN INJARABIAN'S
DEPORTATION AND
ESCAPE TO FREEDOM
(1915-1921)

© Gomidas Institute 2014

anxious to meet us. We told them how we made our way to this place, after enduring so much suffering. The youngest one whispered to us, "Do not trust this man, who has planned to cut your throats! Do not follow him!" We did not want to believe it was true, since the Kurd could have already slaughtered us while walking. In any case, we felt we could not leave him, as we did not know anyone else who could help us. He had led us this far and we had to follow him. It was in that spirit of sadness and resignation that we continued on our way. After leaving the village, the Kurd stopped the donkey and made us dismount. Then, he pulled two watermelons from his saddlebag which we shared together. We were satisfied and the donkey's load lightened. It was then that he proposed that Margaret replace me on the animal's back, while he and I would go on foot. But she refused and we continued on our road, as before.

We were some distance away from the village, which was already hidden by a hill when, losing his graciousness, he commanded that we get down. He pulled out a large cutlass and started to sharpen it saying, "Now, I'm going to kill you." My sister was crying, my mother was overwhelmed, and I thought I could flee to get some help, but felt bound to stay close to them. The Kurd grabbed me by the collar and made me undress. My mother was next. He only allowed us to keep one short frock for clothing and the two of us stood there, almost naked. Still threatening with his large knife, he then forced my desperate sister onto the back of the donkey. She was crying and calling to us, "My dear sweet mommy, my loving little brother, we'll meet again soon." To comfort her, I screamed, "Sister, you go and we'll soon catch up with you!" We were separated in this manner only after a few days of reunion. Until now, we had been spared from death. My sister had saved us at the price of her own life. My mother was on the ground, practically naked, her eyes void of expression – almost strange-looking, having witnessed her daughter's disappearance.

I approached her and proposed that we return to the village where we had just left. I was thinking of the Armenian ladies who had warned us. But my mother refused to follow me, "No, my son . . . you . . . go . . . I'll . . . die . . . here." But I managed to raise her from the ground. Very slowly and painfully, we headed back to the village where a small group of people gathered at the sight of our misfortune. A Kurd stepped forward and handed a garment to my mother so she could cover herself. The young Armenian woman reminded us of her advice and warning, and blamed us for our foolishness. The Kurd finally took us to his home, served us some soup and provided a mattress on the floor for us. Such generosity still would have moved me today, if I had not found out that he had raped my mother that very night, and taken her as a second spouse. Later, he admitted that he admired her for her beauty and wealth, since she had gold teeth in her mouth. As ignorant as he was, he believed it was a sign of dignity.

Three days afterwards, he led us all the way to a house in ruins. He left a mattress and a blanket on the floor and abandoned us in the utmost destitution and said, "From now on, you'll both sleep here." Realizing how sick my mother was and knowing how many exiles were dying of typhoid and dysentery – diseases my mother had probably caught – he had thought it safer to get rid of us in this manner. However, once a day, he would come to look after us and bring a piece of bread, which I can still visualize. It was a type of thick pancake, baked on a sheet of metal, which was heated, for lack of better combustible, with goat and cow dung. At each of his visits, my mother would implore him to put an end to her sufferings and kill her, but without answering, he would look at both of us with a mixed expression of surprise and sorrow. He would leave us the bread and return to the village. I would eat the bread but my mother would not. She was only thirsty, very thirsty. I would go and fetch water at the village well, using an old tin container I found. I had to wait for someone to come and draw some water from a bucket or a sheepskin in order to fill up my container. It was impossible to pull water from the well on my own. Besides being deep, it was very rudimentary, with a large lip and a central pulley – but no rope! Everyone brought their own rope and returned home with it.

A few days went by following the same pattern: the puzzled visit of the Kurd, my mother's pleas which she repeated in vain, the daily bread, and the stops at the well. I was able to endure this way of life without complaints, and suffered only because of my mother's desire to die.

One morning, I woke up in a peaceful silence. For once my mother rested and she was still sleeping. Reassured, I got up and moved, making no noise. Just then, the Kurd arrived for his daily morning visit and called her as usual. No answer. He came close to her, looked at her, and turning towards me he said, "Your mother is dead!" I refused to believe him. I thought that death was a struggle against the unknown, and that no one should die so calmly – without a fight. "No, my mother is not dead. She is still sleeping," I told him. He repeated, "No, your mother is dead – dead!" Then, I turned myself towards her and I shook her. She wasn't moving, and it occurred to me that truly, someone could actually die like that. "Yes," I said without denial, "she is dead. She has abandoned me." The Kurd stared at me without a word. Who was going to take care of me? What would become of me? Who was I going to live with? I was completely alone. The Kurd tied a rope around my mother's feet and pulled and dragged her body further into a gorge. He told me he left her there so that jackals and dogs would not devour her.

When my mother was taken away from me, I said to myself, "My sister saved us but . . ." and no other word came out of my mouth. My whole body started shaking and my teeth clenched. The Kurd saw my condition. He took my hand and led me to a sort of barn. He said, "Stay here until you recover." I stayed in this state of semi-consciousness for quite some time, repeating to myself, "My sister saved us but . . ."

VI

Many days later, the Kurd took me to his home, a grotto at the top of the hill, where he lived with his family and cattle. The neighborhood consisted of several other families dwelling in grottos. I looked around, bewildered, because I never could have imagined people living this way. Although there was only one exit, his grotto consisted of two distinctive parts: on one side lived the people and on the other side were the animals. I stood still next to him, while he was making the cows move inside the area reserved for them. When the last one went in, he gestured to me to enter and showed me inside. I walked in alone and he closed the door of the shed behind me. The place had no opening to let the light in and I found myself in complete darkness. I stretched out my arms like a blind person to protect my body from the animals, which I could feel breathing and moving around me. I finally felt the wall of the grotto, leaned against it, slid down to the ground and sat. I was physically and emotionally exhausted, unable to formulate a thought or to express any feelings at all. I fell asleep.

In the morning, there was light once again for me and the animals. My master spoke Turkish, a language I understood. Pointing to a nearby hill, he ordered me to take his thirty goats to pasture. All he gave me was a stick. Wearing only a short garment to cover me, barefoot, without a hat, and with an empty stomach – I left with my flock. In case of a wolf attack, I was instructed to scream, "Ooel, ooel, ooel!" at the top of my lungs. It was the password used by the village people to call for help. I lived this type of life for several days in a row: I ate poorly, spent the nights in the dark shed, and in the morning, led my goats to the hill.

One day, my master's seventeen or eighteen-year-old son asked me if I wanted to become a Muslim. He could hardly speak Turkish and since I didn't understand the question, I did not reply. He called me and said, "I am going to turn you into a Muslim so you can be one of us."

"What is a Muslim?" I asked. "What does he do?"

He replied, "He does what we do."

"What do you do? I don't know anything yet."

"You'll see, you'll learn how to become a Muslim." And he walked away.

The next day, he made me sit on a big rock in front of him. I could see some donkeys grazing in a field below, bordered by a stretch of ripe wheat. He saw them, too. He turned his head towards me and my initiation began. He spoke in Kurdish, a language I did not understand well. He said, "Tell me, do you want to become a Muslim or stay the son of a *giavour*? (Kurdish for "infidel") You must become a Muslim." I looked at him, stunned. I did not understand a word of the conversation. What should I say, since I did not know what the word *Muslim* meant? He insisted, "You will say, *Eshedoullah ha ilaha, ilallah.*"

I must point out that in Turkish, the word for "donkey" is pronounced *eshek.* I often had to bring back donkeys that were playing in the crops. Therefore, I thought he was trying to teach me a common expression that could be helpful in my work – but that his translation was in poor Turkish. I was convinced he was talking about the donkeys and to please him, I said, "*Esheki, ha esheki.*" Immediately, he slapped me and yelled with rage, "*Lo erzekerek* (dishonorable man)!"

His father, who was sitting nearby, smoking his pipe, did not interfere but his face darkened. Fortunately, my goats were moving astray and I ran after them with tears rolling down my face. I wondered what the word *Muslim* meant. What was the connection between donkey and *Muslim*? Trembling, I went to fetch the donkey without a word, fastened his rope to a rock, and took my goats to pasture. Several days later, the son called me back and said, "Let's repeat and see, *"Eshe doullah . . . ilaha . . ."* I answered what I understood, *"Esheki, ha, esheki, esheki . . ."* Suddenly, a storm of slaps fell on my face, his eyes ablaze with anger. Once again, he insisted that I repeat the same phrase, but I was unable to master it.

The next day, my master spoke to me to find out why I did not want to become a Muslim. "I don't want," I said, not understanding what it meant. He was holding a log in his hand. He threw it at me and spat at the same time, and I dodged both. That day, I was not beaten, but left alone and I finally found some peace. When his wife and children saw me the next day, they marked a line across their throats with their fingers, a sign of disapproval. I still did not understand, and continued to live in total ignorance, amidst their general displeasure and condemnation.

One day, my master's wife and one of her neighbors were standing at the entrance of the grotto in an animated conversation. His wife kept repeating the relentless throat-cutting gesture. I could hear the word *Muslim* mentioned several times. When the old lady looked at me with tearful eyes, I finally understood: because I did not understand what the word meant, my repeated refusal to become a *Muslim* was directly connected to the sacrificial gesture.

That night, as soon as my master returned, I immediately said, "I became a Muslim." He looked at me and kissed me – the first time a Kurd had ever kissed me! He then asked, "Can you say *Eshedoullah ha ilaha, ilallah*?" I remained speechless, with tears filling up in my eyes, but my mind opened up entirely. I understood my mistake and the reason why I had been so harshly beaten. This magical formula had nothing to do with donkeys. My master then told me, while resting his hand on my shoulder, "Well, we'll teach you."

The next day, I could see that his son no longer felt hostile towards me. Instead, he looked at me, shook my hand and said, "*Eshedoullah ha ilaha, ilallah.*" This time, I repeated the redeeming sentence without making any mistakes and he was overjoyed. However, I still had not understood its full meaning and implications. I could only notice faces opening up at my approach and I kept repeating the formula with pride, hoping to gain some favors out of it. Every morning, I repeated, "*Eshedoullah ha ilaha, ilallah*" and I well understood that I had become a Muslim. I was then able to benefit from a certain type of consideration from my master and his family, and we all lived on better terms.

However, I was not really at peace with myself. I started to constantly feel troubled and hurt inside. In my mind, I could see my city and peaceful home, I would relive the days spent with my family, surrounded by my loving parents. My brothers and sisters would reappear vividly in my mind. I remembered the Sundays of my childhood, when my father would hold my hand and take me to church; then, the deportation, the separation, the sufferings, the atrocities, and the loss of all the people I cherished. All these pictures were unfolding in front of my eyes and I felt I was living in another world, a world that did not resemble mine. I didn't know who I was anymore, what *Muslim* meant, why *etche* was not *eshek*. These thoughts brought upon me a kind of madness and I became sick in a strange way, repeating to myself, "Mother, why have you abandoned me? Why didn't you take me with you so I could die a Christian?"

At night, when I was confined to solitude and darkness, a violent impulse was pushing me out of the grotto. For several hours, I would wander aimlessly around the dwellings, spasms running through my body. I would hide behind rocks and dig holes feverishly. I felt hunted down, followed, threatened. I would see my enemies' faces and daggers glowing in the dark. My master's son would sometimes follow me with a knife in his hand, thinking I might run away. Who knows if the urge to flee was not the real cause of my sickness? Weary, I finally calmed down and would return to my grotto next to the oxen, where my place to sleep was much like a manger. My agonies vanished with the morning light. This state of madness lasted many weeks, without anyone else noticing it. The adults finally realized how sick I was, but at the same time, my master became ill. He thought I had given him my disease. When he recovered, he called me, put his donkey's halter in my hand, and told me we were leaving. He was dressed to travel.

We had only walked a few steps, passing in front of our neighbor's grotto, when the neighbor came out to his doorstep to meet us. He and my master kept talking for some time, while I waited, holding the donkey. All of a sudden, my master grabbed the halter out of my hand and pointing to the neighbor, declared, "Now, our brother is your dad." I left my first master in this way, after a period of three months. I watched him walk away with his donkey and I said to myself, "*Eshek* or *Eshe* . . . I am a Muslim, but God, my God, tell me what is it to be a Muslim?"

VII

My second Kurdish master and his wife spoke proper Turkish. He was quite tall and slim, with a gray beard. His name was Ibrahim Bekir. The couple had a seven-year-old daughter named Guley, which means "rose" in Turkish. They were poor and the wife argued with her husband about why he had agreed to take in a *giavour*, who would be a burden – and a sick one, too. She looked at me with hostility. Her husband did not give in to her arguments and listed all the services I would be able to render as soon as I recovered.

I learned from him that my previous master had planned to lead me to Suruj, a city now located near the Syrian border. Suruj, with its swamps, was a real concentration camp for the Armenians. They were dying every day by the dozens and under the most agonizing conditions. Ibrahim Bekir's intervention had kept me from perishing in that way. I felt deep gratitude towards this man, who probably had saved my life, and so I bowed my head.

He asked what my name was and I answered, "Papken." My name sounded incredible to him, and it was impossible for him to pronounce it. He asked me to repeat it, which I did. He made several attempts to say it again, without much success, causing him to burst into laughter. He came to the conclusion that Papken was not a real name, and that I needed another one – a Muslim name, of course. So he asked me to choose between Abdullah and Aziz. I thought the latter sounded closer to my native language. So I decided to be called Aziz. He made me enter his grotto which was not large, but he set aside a small place for me, just enough to lie down on straw between two stones.

My new master had an older brother, who lived at the bottom of the hill, in a kind of a small village community. He lived there with his family and an Armenian woman, who was probably at his service. In fact, this was the same woman who had warned my mother, sister, and me that it was dangerous to trust the Kurd, who later took Margaret away. Their cone-shaped house was constructed with a mixture of mud and finely cut straw, which resembled sun-dried brick. He was not as poor as his brother. Close to his home, was a sloping grotto, large and deep, which was used both as a dwelling for a Kurdish family and a shelter for horses, donkeys, and oxen. It also served as a place to store cheese, litter for animals, and materials. I used to go there quite often to do some occasional chores. It mainly gave me a chance to visit Mariam, the Armenian lady, who was kind and supportive, and who spoke in my mother tongue, helping me to endure my harsh, lonely existence.

One week later, my master called me and told me, "I am leaving for five to six days with my donkeys to fetch some wheat." I already understood that my master was making a living out of this trade. I worried about his absence, because his wife disliked me and I was afraid that she could harm me. In fact, as soon as he left, she drove me out of her grotto. She ordered me to go and move out further in a small, rocky pit. She gave me some straw and an old, ragged bag in which to sleep. I obeyed but I was frightened to be on my own in such a remote place. Every morning, I would get out of my hole and sit in front of my master's grotto. Little Guley would bring me a piece of bread and I would live off it all day long, like a beggar, waiting for my allowance. In order to drink water, I had to go to the village's only well, which was quite a distance away. On the way there, I would pass in front of the house where Mariam lived. She would give me some water when she saw me, and that would save me from going any further.

Finally, my master returned. He found out about my condition, rebuked his wife severely, and restored my place among them. However, whenever her husband went away, she would take advantage of the situation and throw me out. Months went by. One day, my master's brother left the village with his family and my friend Mariam, and moved to another one. Immediately, my master took possession of his brother's house and provided a place – just for me – in the large slanted grotto next door. From that point on, it became my retreat – my kingdom! For the first time in a long time, I experienced a kind of happiness.

Another family, already living in one section of the grotto, had two sons, who were my own age, and who became my playmates. I was a foreigner to them. Since I did not know their language very well, I would express myself mostly with gestures and we would make fun of one another. We became good friends.

My duties consisted of feeding the oxen, cleaning the litter and the stable, and sieving the small pieces of straw. I was at peace, I was gaining some weight, I had shelter from the cold, and I had friends. I was coming back to life. I learned how to speak Kurdish with my mates. I would joke heartily with those who could speak Turkish, like me, aware of the prestige I had gained in their eyes. Besides, wasn't I Aziz and a Muslim?

My master's wife was the only one who continued calling me by my Armenian name, and she mispronounced it, too. She wanted to prove to everyone I was still a *giavour*, so they would not forget. Some Kurds would eventually say that my name was Aziz and I had become a Muslim. She would retort that I was undeserving of the name, and that it was sinful to give such a name to a *giavour*. "But he is a Muslim," they answered, "He can say, '*Eshedoullah ha ilaha, ilallah*'." "Maybe, but he doesn't pronounce it properly! He still says it in a *giavour* way." The others told me, "Come on, say '*Eshedoullah ha ilaha, ilallah*,' so she can hear it herself." With an air of importance, I would say, "*Eshedoullah ha ilaha, ilallah Mohammedi Avdouhoura Resoul Allah Allah Ekber!*"

The Kurds would nod their heads in approval. All I saw were friendly faces smiling at me. They all told my mistress I had become a real Muslim and I was thus deserving of my name, Aziz. And then, to show me some kind indulgence, they called me Azo, a nickname that remained with me.

VIII

There were four or five wealthy families in this village. Each owned at least one hundred or more sheep. As I was growing up quickly, becoming stronger, and working with spirit, some of them asked me to leave my master, who was very poor. They wanted me to work for them and in return, offered nice lodging and good meals, including enticements, such as butter and yogurt. They promised me everything in abundance. "Your master is so poor, he doesn't even have bread to eat," they would say. The thought of quitting and accepting their offers was very appealing, especially since my master's wife was so harsh and barely fed me. However, I was afraid my master would look for me everywhere and severely punish me for being ungrateful. As desperately tempting as the promises of butter and yogurt were, didn't I owe him my life?

The son of one of these rich families, a tall, strong fellow, called me one morning, took me by the arm, and led me to the well. Hundreds of sheep, all gathered together in one compact herd, were waiting there. What had happened? The wooden pulley had come undone and had fallen to the bottom of the well. He and some others thought that if they could tie a rope around my waist and lower me down, I could retrieve it. They claimed they would reward me with wonderful food, such as butter and yogurt, if I agreed to help. I was hungry and rejoiced at the prospect of this tasty food. I approached the well to evaluate its depth, but as I leaned over the edge, I saw neither the pulley nor the surface of the water, just a wide-open, bottomless, black hole. I refused to help and cried, "I won't go!" Although I tried to escape, several men grabbed me forcefully and tied a rope with a tight knot around my waist. There I was, hanging in the well, holding a rough rope between my hands.

I yelled, "I don't want to go down!" Laughing gleefully, they replied that I had to make a special effort to earn my butter and yogurt. In truth, I had forgotten about the reward. I was only focused on moving down deeper and deeper into the black, echoing pit. I soon realized it was useless to cry or implore. I could hear them screaming from the top, "Azo, let us know when you touch the water!" It was hard to see anything in the dark, but finally, I noticed a sheet of water beneath me, shining like a mirror, that seemed to come closer. Thinking the water was within reach and my trouble at its end, I yelled, "That's it!" Immediately, they stopped lowering me. Then, stretching my body, I tried to touch the surface of the water, but I was still too far away and shouted, "Some more!" They loosened the rope and I finally skimmed the surface of the water with my foot, making me shudder. I yelled out, "Arrived!" The well was very wide at the bottom, and the pulley was floating, but out of my reach. I suddenly became frightened, but it was necessary to get to it and bring it back, no matter what. That was what they expected of me and I had to succeed, in spite of all the difficulties. I didn't dare ask to be lowered a touch more, because I feared being immersed, so I used a lot of imagination and skill to achieve my task. Using my feet as contact and support, and then as oars, I finally managed to swing and grab the pulley. I happily yelled, "Pull me up!" They started to pull and my ascent began, under their awkward and irregular arm motions. As I was lifted back up, my shoulders and head got knocked around against the wall, while I held the pulley tightly against me.

At last, I reached daylight once again, and they told me to hand over the pulley. I stretched out my arm and feeling that someone's hands had gotten hold of it, I let it go. Alas, as luck would have it, one of the men's unsteady hands dropped it and the pulley fell back to the bottom of the well! Of course, they made me go back down. But this time, I wasn't scared. I knew I would be pulled up again and not left at the bottom of the well. Having learned my lesson, I held the pulley tightly against my body and I got out of the well with it, trusting no one. They were all standing there, watching me and laughing. Whenever the pulley happened to fall to the bottom of the well, I was always summoned to go and fetch it – no matter where I was or what I was doing. I was afraid they would harass me, so I carried out this chore each time. I did it without any hope of reward, since they never did deliver the promised butter and yogurt!

My master heard about this situation and decided to intervene, but first, he had to catch them in the act. Thus, one day, he arrived at the very moment I was being pulled out of the well. He flew into a rage, saying that I belonged to him and he was feeding me. I was under his protection and under his orders, and no one besides him had the right to use me. The others were stunned by his intervention, thinking that such a level of anger was not justified. They commented, "Why give such consideration to a *giavour*?" My master took me by the hand and walked away. From that day on, I knew I had a protector and I felt invigorated. I could now refuse to go down the well without fearing any retaliation. In fact, it never happened again. I knew deep inside I was much better off living with my poor master in a grotto, than with rich owners, who had butter and yogurt!

IX

My first master died. His family and friends accompanied him on his last journey. His body, carried in the arms of some of the men, was only wrapped in a shroud. This is because at the time, coffins did not exist in the country. As they passed by, I remembered the time he wanted to see me, a few weeks after he had given me to my present master. I found him in a gloomy and almost threatening mood. He was crouched on his heels with his back turned to his grotto, and his face turned up towards the sun. He spoke in a distressed voice and said, "Your mother gave me her disease!" I did not say a word as I stood before him. I then walked away.

While watching the funeral procession, I thought that justice had been rendered for his deeds. The water and bread he had provided had not come free, as my mother had to pay the high price of her honor – and perhaps, her life. He had welcomed us in our extreme deprivation, but took advantage of our suffering and weakness. Today, he was punished. The feeling of retribution penetrated my heart.

My worries had begun to fade with time. I could speak Kurdish almost fluently. I was often told I had become a true Kurd. In reality, I was a dirty, ragged-looking child, with a bare head and bare feet. The only piece of clothing I had was a tattered, knee-length shirt, blackened by dirt. This same garment also served as my towel and handkerchief. Around my waist was a string knotted so tightly, that it was impossible to untie.

There was an Armenian boy about my age, who lived close to our home. He was taller and sturdier than me. His master was wealthy and owned sheep and cattle. He wore shoes, was rather well-dressed, and well-fed. He did not know Turkish and refused to speak Armenian with me. He only spoke Kurdish. He was a shepherd, like me, and I was eager to go with him on the hill where his herd was grazing, but my master did not own any sheep. Finally one day, we took our masters' oxen to pasture and I hoped that this would be an opportunity to get to know him better. I asked where he was from, about his family, his brothers' and sisters' names, his story. He replied to all my questions in Kurdish, giving the same answer: that his name was Hamed Ali and that he was a Muslim. I could see I was annoying him. Had he forgotten his childhood, the exodus, our dead? We were two deported Armenian boys having two Kurd masters and because of his attitude, we could not become friends. The fact that we were not able to be mates, with all that we had in common, was really psychologically frustrating for me. I felt so tormented by this that I started to work harder to forget him.

My master left on another expedition with several neighbors to a city named Birejik, located on the banks of the Euphrates River. When he arrived in the city, he encountered a squad of gendarmes and was officially drafted by the Turkish army, which was in need of men. Hence, all Kurdish men who were between the ages of 18 and 50 were in danger of one day being involuntarily recruited as Turkish soldiers.

One of my master's friends managed to escape and came to deliver the bad news to his wife. When he saw me, he said, "Your dad is a soldier!" This news provoked a shock and I started to cry. Actually, all my thoughts and emotions were focused on my real father, because in my naivety, I still could not imagine he could be gone forever. Even though my common sense told me otherwise, I still hoped that he would come one day to fetch me and take me away from my Kurdish masters. Thus, I wept copiously and people thought I was grieving my master's fate. When he returned home a few weeks later, he found out how much I had wept. He looked at me closely, asking me why I had been so afflicted, and why I did not think he would be able to escape. I did not answer, wanting to hide the truth. "This *giavour* must love you so much to cry over a Kurd who became a soldier," people said. Grateful and flattered, he began calling me his son. I did the same and called him "Daddy." Since that day, because of this misunderstanding, a deeper affection developed between us.

His wife was getting visibly fatter and I didn't understand why. One afternoon, when we were both working in the field, he told me that his wife was very big now and she would soon become a mother. I was so obsessed by food, I told him I thought she was big because she ate too much. At my age, I did not know how babies were born, as my parents had always told me stories on the subject. A few days later, indeed, a baby boy was born, named Ghader and my master was really happy.

Some time after, he had to leave again, and I became sick. During his absence, one of his brothers-in-law, who had fled the army, paid a visit. He was convinced *giavours* were responsible for the war and did not hide his repugnance. He was a stout man – a ruffian, in fact – rough and dirty, who had quite a terrible look. On his belt was a dagger. One very hot day, and in spite of my weakness, he asked me to come to the well with him to get water, and to undo the rope. I obeyed, taking the rope and followed him without any questions. However, I was anxious about where he was taking me and what his intentions were. While we were walking, he said that the day before, he had seen a large cavity in the ground while on the hill. Curious, he had bent down to look and dropped his pipe into the bottom of the pit. The opening was too narrow for him and he thought I could climb down to fetch it. I stopped worrying and thought the task was easy to achieve. Hadn't I been down the village well before?

When we reached the place, which was very remote, I saw a small opening in the ground with rocks at the bottom. I first believed I could venture in it without any risk, since the hole, even though quite deep, had no water. A sound coming out from the bottom of the cavity drew my attention. While I bent forward, I noticed a large nest of intertwined snakes whistling and moaning – like babies – their eyes shining and mouths wide open! The man asked me to go and fetch some rocks. I handed them to him one by one and he violently threw them down on the moving and wailing mass of snakes. After a short while, we could not hear a thing. He called me and pointed to his pipe. He ordered me to climb down. Terrified by snakes, I vigorously refused to do it. I argued that the rope we had was worn out, which was the truth. The Kurd lost his temper. Enraged, he screamed, then pulled out his dagger and kept hitting me brutally with the back of the blade. I thought my bones were breaking apart. I cried and yelled out in despair. I thought I was living my last suffering and that my time had come. I thus said, "I'd rather die from the blows of a dagger than from snake bites!" After a short struggle, he let me go, but the blade had penetrated my skin in several places. He called me a dirty *giavour*. "If you didn't belong to my sister, I would have killed you after getting my pipe and thrown your body into the pit to let the snakes finish you! You worthless *giavours*! You don't even deserve to die like dogs!" I left in tears.

I returned to the village. The violence and trauma I had just experienced took a heavy toll on my health, which was already considerably weakened. For a few days I became terribly sick. My whole body was shaking and my teeth were chattering. I was like a mad person. If I was seated, everything would swirl around me. The walls and objects were all moving in front of my eyes in a hallucinatory dance. I felt better when lying on my back. In a state of semi-consciousness, I would see my home, my parents, my brothers and sisters, and I thought I could fly to meet them. I would then stand up and stretch my arms like a bird would do with its wings. But because I would remain on the ground, my agitation would return.

My mistress was indifferent to my distress and disorder. An old lady from the neighborhood took pity and nursed me. She would wrap a wet rag around my head and stay next to me a few hours a day. She would serve me a beverage that was supposed to cure me. Just her contact alone soothed me, because she acted like a mother. Thanks to her prayers and comfort, I regained my spirits and my serenity. When my master came back from his expedition, I began to recover and gain some strength.

X

I had become a familiar face in the village and a lot of people now paid attention to me. Often, Kurds would encourage me to wrestle with the children of my own age and would enjoy watching us. I used to throw them to the ground, which made my master proud. Each time I would knock a boy down, he would shout, "*Lo, Azo noney ke too doukhi halalley!*" ("You, Azo, you well deserve the bread I give you!") My success in the village was related to the fact that I appeared very cultured to them. My knowledge and my cleverness made up for my frail appearance and they enjoyed speaking Turkish to me. I knew a lot of jokes in that language that made them laugh. Even the people who could not fully understand were entertained by my stories and would show me some respect, mixed with gaiety. Sometimes, when gathered under a tent, they would call me:

O Merhabo, Aziz, hal keyf etde? (Hello Aziz, How are you?)

Erendem lo. (Very well)

Elhamdoullah. (Thank God)

Say '*Eshe doullah*' so every one can hear you.

Eshe doullah ha ilaha illallah.

Great, Aziz. Since you have become a Muslim, we'll circumcize you when the Iman comes around. Now, speak to us in *giavour*.

Vallahee. (I've forgotten)

Tell us how the *giavours* bury their dead.

I could not reply to these words. Since I had witnessed death so closely, it had a very solemn and poignant meaning to me. I did not want to say anything stupid on the subject, fearing their mockeries. Then, an old Kurd, assuming an air of importance, got me out of trouble by telling this story:

"One day a *giavour* died. Two priests all dressed in black came near the corpse and said, '*Djem, djem, djem, djem* . . .' Then, they picked him up to carry away towards a hole so deep that water reached the surface. Then, two men came, grabbed the dead, one by the feet, the other by the hands and flung him into the hole, with his face against the ground . . ."

I listened to the old Kurd's story with disbelief, because only criminals were buried that way. The other Kurds, who were quite ignorant, looked amazed and then laughed heartily. He continued:

"The two priests repeated, '*Djem, djem, djem, djem* . . .' and they ordered soil and big stones to be thrown over the corpse until the hole was totally covered."

Everybody turned around and looked at me.

"Is this true, Aziz?"

"Yes, it is," I answered calmly.

"Why do they do that?"

"*Efendim* (Sirs), so jackals don't come to dig up the dead, who are sacred. If they did otherwise, the dead would quickly become the jackals' prey, as it is for your dead, for example."

"*Lo erzegherkh!* (Boy with no honor!) How can you say that?"

It was a good answer I had given and I was proud of it, since the men were debating among themselves. Some agreed with me willingly; others, offended, were angry and accused me of threatening their honor. Some just laughed. However, before responding, I quickly made sure there was an empty space behind me, where I could escape to – in case of danger!

During this heated discussion, a man arrived on his horse. He was an older Kurd of importance, richly dressed, and everyone stood up to welcome him. "*Merhabo*" (Hello) could be heard from all sides. He was a cousin of the man who owned the tent, where we were gathered. He dismounted and asked me to fetch some water for his horse. I obeyed, took the harness, and tried to ride the horse to the well. The man said, "Do not ride this horse. He is fiery and mean, and he could thrust you to the ground." Pretending I had not heard anything, I moved a few steps forward and tried to raise myself up on the horse's back. Everybody screamed, "Do not ride, the horse is crazy!" This time, compelled to obey, I pulled the animal all the way to the well. I drew some water and the horse drank plentifully, because the heat was intense. When he was satiated, I mounted him and there I was, arriving in front of the audience, superb like a pasha. They all looked at me, surprised, saying good-heartedly, "Terrible child, you rode it anyway!" I can still hear myself answer, "Now that this horse has drunk, he has become reasonable." And everybody burst out laughing.

The rider, a man who was respected because of his age and wealth, found me entertaining and started taking an interest in me. After I had tied up his horse, he made me sit next to him and began asking me questions:

"Where are you from?"

"I'm from Amasia."

"I just came from there."

I told him my parents' name and he assured me he knew them well. I stared at this man, who was bringing fresh news from my dear country and perhaps from my loved ones. In fact, my father knew a lot of people, precisely rich farmers like this one, and on the occasion of great trade fairs, we had up to fifty or sixty guests from all over sitting at our table.

He asked me what my father's profession was. "A butcher," I answered. "Yes, I know him, I know him very well. He was wearing a fez on his head." And the whole audience laughed loudly because in my country, every man wore a fez. I understood he had tricked me, and changing my expression, I retorted with a straight face, "But I also know your father well." He looked at me dumbfounded, not understanding how a young boy like me could have met his parents, when he himself was quite old. The others were wondering, too. And without giving anyone time to react, I added, "He wore a big mustache and a beard, exactly like you!" A roar of laughter broke out. "*Aferim*, Azo!" (Well done, Azo!)

Whenever the opportunity arose, I would participate in their joking around and when they spoke seriously, I would answer seriously. Thanks to my master's kindness and affection for me, I had the opportunity to be included in these entertaining moments among the village Kurds. Most of them were uneducated and many could not even count at all; whereas I could read and count not only in Armenian, but quite correctly in Turkish, too.

XI

As I already noted, my master was extremely poor. His situation became even worse on some recent business trips, when two of his four donkeys were stolen. He was then compelled to stop his trade because the two remaining donkeys could not provide sufficient help – and he could not afford to replace the stolen ones. I continued taking our donkeys to pasture with those of my mates. With a dozen animals, I was feeling well and at peace. It was the work I preferred.

But I noticed my master was looking for a solution to our miserable fate. He finally decided to leave the village of Aghmughara. One day, he left with the oxen. The following day it was my turn, along with the two donkeys carrying all our goods, little Guley, and my mistress, who carried her newborn baby on her back. I escorted the convoy and was in a melancholy state. I felt very sad leaving this place, where I had lived for one year and which knew my story. After all, this was where my mother had died. I could feel the last ties with my family and my past breaking away.

The village where we were going, Mederbaz, was a five to six-hour walk. My master was meeting his older brother and two younger ones, who I did not know. On my arrival, I started looking for Mariam, the Armenian woman who had known my mother. "She has gone to Suruj," I was told with indifference. "She must be dead by now." I felt a deep sorrow, a void inside me, and I had no one to share my sadness with. I then learned that two young Armenians, a brother and a sister, were living at my master's younger brother's place. I waited impatiently for the opportunity to meet them.

At Mederbaz, there were no grottos. The village was quite small and included a few houses roughly built in a type of brick. A high mountain rose up in front of the village. We lived in one of those houses near a well. We had a few goats and we farmed our fields to provide for the food. This situation was the result of an agreement. The goats did not belong to my master, but he was feeding them and making them grow bigger. At each birth, he would share the kids, or newborns with the owner of the fields. So I became a goatkeeper. One morning, as I was keeping my small herd, I met the young Armenian boy whom I had heard about. He was also keeping his master's goats, which was a much larger herd. After that, we would meet every day and became good friends. He was slightly older than me, mature, and his memories were still very vivid. He and his sister came from Birejik, located along the Euphrates River, the very city where my master would go for his business. In fact, we were not far from there. My new friend did not speak any Kurdish but was quite fluent in Turkish. He was always sad and would repeat tirelessly, "O *Fellec, Fellec,* what painful ordeals you made us experience! What misery you put us through!" I asked him who was *Fellec* and he told me, "You don't know who *Fellec* is? He is the one who put us in this misery." I told myself that if I met *Fellec*, I would kill him. I found out later that *Fellec* was *fate* and there was nothing you could do against it.

Days and weeks went by. We stayed on the mountain each day until sunset and we were famished. One day my friend, furious, was threatening the sun screaming, "I've been watching you for two hours and you haven't moved out of your place yet. Go to set, disappear behind the mountain so we can go eat and rest!" I had never heard the sun summoned like that before. Finally, the sun disappeared behind the mountain and we returned to our homes, devouring the allowance our masters were willing to give us.

The rations, already quite meager, started to diminish especially when my master was gone or when I came late at night. I dared not complain to him. I just could not think about anything but food and I started to steal. First, I stole a little food, but later, much more. I was hungry, constantly hungry.

My master, his wife, the children, and I all slept in the same room. Their bed was a woolen mattress set on the ground and covered with a blanket, while mine was a bag in a corner. The goats and the two donkeys stayed in the adjoining room and the larger cattle in the next one. We slept in total darkness, except for the pale glimmer of the night that entered the room through the wide open door. At night, when everybody seemed to be asleep, I would get up and without a sound, swallow all the leftovers, yogurt, dairy products, cooked herbs – whatever was left in our cooking pans. When she arose in the morning, my mistress discovered the theft and wondered who could have done such a thing. I said, "I haven't seen a thing. It's certainly the cat." Eager to find out, she placed the pots near where she slept, almost against her head. She thought the cat would not dare go up there or if he did, she could also catch him by surprise. One particular night, I decided to take a risk. I rose up quietly from my corner and crawled on my belly with agility while fumbling around. I reached the container filled with cooked herbs and carefully raised the lid. It happened to be the very moment my master chose to go out to relieve himself! I was left in the pitch black of night, holding the lid within the breath of my sleeping mistress! I quickly thought over this difficult situation. I was afraid of making any noise by putting the lid down, but cats cannot raise lids and I had to set it back. I had to do so at all costs and crawl back to my place. Unfortunately, my hurried hand knocked over another pot and all went flying, which caused a big commotion. I ran to my corner and waited. My master and his wife, unable to see in the total darkness, believed the cat did it and said "shoo, shoo . . ." I, in turn, pretended to wake up with a start and did the same. I then picked up a piece of wood and threw it forcefully toward the pots and pans. There was another crash and more fussing. I screamed, "The cat has just run over me!" "Do you think he left?" asked my master. "Yes, he fled outdoors!"

I had been saved by darkness. In those remote places, the light of the stars was all there was. Even the time was divided in moons.

XII

The famine was intensifying. The crops had been particularly poor that year. On the other hand, the Turkish gendarmes were carrying off all the supplies and were busy looking for wheat. The Kurds, who did not own a shelter to house their harvest, were burying their wheat to hide it from the searches. They were digging large trenches, two to three meters deep, and packing the wheat there. It was protected on the bottom and sides by a thin layer of finely cut straw. Another layer covered the top. All trading of cereal was interrupted. My master had only half a bag of flour and half a bag of pre-cooked hand-crushed wheat left for his whole family. We had to live on it for four to five months or until the next harvest. The bread was now made of a dough of cooked herbs and flour, and day after day, the proportion of cooked herbs became larger.

I remember one morning, when I was alone at home with Guley, I discovered a large wooden container in which there was yogurt saved for the evening dinner. Several times, I hid from

Guley and took some of the yogurt with my fingers – and I caught her doing the same. Without realizing it, the missing portion became quite obvious. At night, my master came back while I was outdoors. He called me. He looked terrible and I felt I was in danger. I walked very slowly towards him. Grabbing my ear and pointing to the container he said:

Who ate this?

Vallahi billahi (I swear it wasn't me)

Gavour, oghlou giavour (Son of an infidel!) If it wasn't you, who was it then? Guley could not have swallowed all this yogurt!

He hit me hard and took me between his legs. He put his hands around my neck and, in a rage, he started to tighten them. After a good amount of screaming and squirming, I succeeded in sliding out of his grip and fled outside. He ran after me throwing big stones. I fell on the ground bleeding, covered with bruises. Some women walking by saw me but did not interfere while stones kept raining on my body. I was blinded by my blood. It was as if I were dead. Finally, my master's rage calmed down. I rose up and dragged myself to the edge of a dry well. There, crouched against a small wall, I started crying bitterly. Some people passing by heard my moaning and thought it was coming from the bottom of the well. They ran to get help. My master finally sent someone to inquire after me and I was taken back to the village. I had been so badly beaten that they expected me to die from the blows. I saw my master's elder brother lecturing him and blaming him vehemently for the savage beating I had endured. But my master's wrath had died down and I understood he regretted his acts of violence. I understood too, that I had deserved a punishment but what else could I do but steal to fight my hunger?

My starvation was becoming more severe. At home, there was nothing left to steal. I was picking up fresh grass and chewing on it to cheat my hunger. I was trying to fill up on it. The goats and

I were grazing together. The contact with leaves and roots was hurting my lips. One day, while I was far from home, an idea came to me. A big goat was giving lots of milk. I grabbed her, laid her on the ground and started to suck her milk voraciously like an infant. I felt comforted and I told myself I would do it again. But my crime did not go unnoticed. In spite of my denials, my mistress observed that the big goat was giving less milk. My initiative had failed. I had to look for something else.

I got into the habit of stealing more and more – and without being punished again. It was bad, I knew it, and a little voice inside me was saying it was sinful – but I was starving. Staying alive was a relentless struggle for me – so I stole each time I had a chance. One day, a woman left her home. She pulled her door behind her without locking it and there she went. I hid and followed her with my eyes as far as possible towards the fields. Then, glancing around rapidly, I pushed the door open and entered her house. I looked for bread but there was not even one crumb. In a corner of her bedroom, I saw a large wooden container used to prepare yogurt, which was covered up with care. I had to act quickly and since there was no spoon around I uncovered the container, knelt down, and dipped my face in it. The milk had barely hardened and was still lukewarm. I gluttonously gulped down long sips without breathing. I put the cover back on the large bowl, washed my face in some dirty water I found, and left. I made sure nobody had noticed anything and did it so quickly that I could still see the lady walking towards the fields. The following day, the lady came to complain to my master and said, "Your boy ate my yogurt!" And my master turned towards me and asked, "You're the one who did it?" "*Vallahi billahi*" (I swear it wasn't me). Seeing my stubbornness in denying it, the lady insulted me, cursed me, and left in a state of blind anger. After her departure, my master said, "*Lo erzekeregh*! (That is your doing!) I know it's you . . . but what's done . . . is done." I kept quiet, still remembering his ferocious beating. However, I felt almost a slight shade of respect in his answer, and came to the conclusion that the more I would steal, the less I would be beaten. But where to go and steal?

XIII

Soon after, I discovered a field where the barley had ripened faster than anywhere else. The grains were filled with a kind of milky liquid. I pruned them in my hands and fed myself with this poor treat. I then began to save a sort of stock: the grains that were picked up the day before were easier to work in my hands and their taste was better. I fed myself this way for several days but it did not last long, because I lost all sense of caution by increasing my ration. Emboldened, I penetrated further inside the field and tore away more and more ears of barley, greatly expanding the boundaries of my plunder. That was when the field owner came, caught me in the very act, and tried to grab me. I ran away, he darted after me, and I yelled with all my strength. My master, hearing my screams, came running to my rescue armed with a strong stick. When he understood what it was all about, he spoke to the man. "What do you want? We are not going to kill him for that!" He then grabbed me by the collar and took me back home. Once more, I was saved, and once more, I was not beaten.

The famine continued to get worse. The farmers were waiting for the barley to ripen. During that period, I was asked by a well-to-do Kurd to keep a dozen lambs for him with my goats. I accepted. My master found out, closed his eyes to it, and did not use it as an excuse to reduce my meal allowance. This lasted about two weeks. I profited a great deal from the extra food. Good for me!

My master had heard that the harvest of the barley had already started in some neighboring areas. He called me and entrusted me with the donkey and a bag to go to the village of Bozdepe. I was to fetch a supply of barley from his friend there, which would allow us to wait until the harvest. Later, when the crops were gathered, he would give it back. "Send him our greetings," said my master, "and watch for thieves and ruffians in that region. They will steal your donkey!"

Early in the morning, I thus left with the animal and the bag. I went as I pleased, sometimes on foot and other times perched on my donkey. The road was long. As I reached the top of a high hill and was about to descend to the bottom of the valley, I noticed a man on the opposite summit riding in my direction. If we met and if by chance he attacked me, calling for help would be in vain, since in this remote place, no one would have come. I then had the idea to climb on my donkey and gallop away. At the same time, I shouted at the top of my voice, "*Sevar hat! Sevar hat!*" and looked terrified. It was the warning call used by the villagers. They would scream it to announce the presence of recruiting officers, riding their horses from one village to the other. At this call, all Kurd men would disappear in a split second and so escape enrollment. But there I was, almost passing the man coming in my direction. His general appearance did not reassure me so I yelled with renewed ardor, "*Sevar hat! Sevar hat!*" while overriding my mount. The man became confused and opened wide his worried eyes, asking, "Where are they?" "They are coming behind me, from the other side of the hill." Without listening any further, the man turned his mount around and soon disappeared. He was a strong fellow with a cruel look in his eyes.

Finally, I arrived at the village of Bozdepe and there, I greeted my master's friend politely. I inquired about his family. I soon realized that the barley was not ripe, no more ripened than ours.

The rumour that the barley had been harvested in the region was false. He offered me a glass of water. I returned home with my donkey and my empty bag, arriving in front of the house before sunset. My master was expecting me with hope. Alas! I did not bring back anything. Disappointed, he counted the three to four weeks we had to wait until the harvest.

After my return and my shrewd response in escaping a possible attack in the hills, my master became more attentive to me. He pitied my constant hunger, since there was nothing to steal anymore. He was also concerned about my health: I was completely eaten up by lice, which were sucking my blood all over my body. The pain was terrible!

I had been wearing an old corn bag made of rough material, which replaced the torn shirt I had since the deportation. The bag was infested with those horrible bugs, which were swarming in profusion. At night, above a fire of cow dung, we each held one end of my bag and heated it up. Then, we would slap it with our hands several times and legions of lice would drop into the fire. There were so many that for a split second the flame was revived. My master would then raise a pensive hand to his beard declaring that he had never seen so many lice in his entire life. As an expert, he gave me this piece of advice: when I was in the meadows on a hot day, I should undress and set my garment on an anthill. And so I did. The ants were delighted to be served live delicious food at their nest and I was happy to have relief from the constant bites. I thanked my master for his help and he said with emotion in his voice, "*Aferim!* (Bravo!) You honor your name Aziz by your thanks." He felt proud that his adopted son showed him gratitude.

At last, after several weeks, my master's wife was able to give us some barley bread. I had worked very hard with my master to gather the precious cereal by hand. Crouched down, we pulled handfuls of the barley with the roots. The grains were then crushed by a hand mill made of two circular grinding stones. As my food allowance increased, I gained back some strength.

However, the harvest was not generous enough and my master decided we needed another bag of flour to be safe. So he sent me to fetch more flour from his mother-in-law, who lived in a neighboring village. After a two-hour walk, I reached the place at sunset. I was advised to wait until morning to go back because of the late hour and all types of danger. I refused, arguing that my master would worry and left with the bag on my shoulder. I walked fast but after an hour, it turned completely dark. I could not see a thing and was almost like a blind person, barely catching a dim sight of the road through the obscurity. I was forced to reduce my speed. Some time after, I reached an intersection of two roads I recognized: the one I was already on and another narrower one, which was a shortcut to my village, by way of the cemetery. I thought it over for a moment and decided to stay on my path, which was wider, better outlined, and easier to distinguish in the dark. Soon after, I noticed a large moving shape ahead of me, coming my way. I held the bag in my hands, ready to defend myself vigorously. It seemed to be a man with a shiny object in his hand and indeed, he was soon close to me. I barely made out other threatening shadows in the dark. The man was armed with a dagger. He stopped me and ordered me to follow him. He took me behind the hill in a remote place where guards were watching over horses. I realized I had come across a gang of thieves. However, I was not too worried. What could they take? I was only a child carrying a bag and wearing rags and lice. The first man started to ask me questions in Kurdish: "*Kouda dari lo?*" (Tell me, where are you going?) "*Ez daremey Mederbaz*" (I'm going to Mederbaz.)"*Koure kei?*" (Who are you the son of?) "*Ez koure Ibrahim Bekirim.*" (I am the son of Ibrahim Bekir.)

He asked me to wait where I was and he would take me back to my village. I had introduced myself as the true son of a Kurd and he was pleased with my answer. If I had confessed my real origin, I would have been murdered on the spot. I was sitting close to the men who were conversing in Turkish. I did not miss a word of their discussion, pretending however to understand nothing. All of a sudden, someone came to declare that a caravan of camels was in sight. They all ran down the hill with their weapons to blockade the road. I remained on the premises with a guard and the horses so that I would not raise an alarm. After some time, they all came back and I understood they had not found a thing to steal. They were full of rage. Before sunrise, they climbed on their horses and I kept walking alongside them. They soon pointed to my village, which could be seen in the early light of the morning, and left me.

Suddenly, some dogs started to bark loudly for no reason. I sat on the ground and waited motionless because I had heard it was the thing to do. The dogs came close to me, circled around me several times, and then went away. I could still hear them barking in the distance. After a while, I stood up stealthily, staggered home, and got to my bed before my whole body started shivering. It lasted all night and the following day. I was in a state of shock. My master had already found the empty bag, but my condition worried him. He let me rest longer than usual. Then, he came and asked, "Son, what's wrong?" I told him the whole story about the darkness, the ruffians, and the dogs. He listened and started laughing, "You are brave! But you should not fear those horsemen who steal bags and money," and he told me a similar story that had happened to him. He added, "You should not worry about the bag either. One more or one less, is not a big deal. God will give it back. But fear is not suitable to a man." It was the first time he had talked to me that way and his last words became impressed in my memory. I was moved and I kissed his hand. "You don't need to, my son. Just be brave and fearless!" was his only answer.

On several occasions, I had planned to leave my master to find a wealthier one, so that I would not have to steal anymore. But after these good words of support, I decided to stay. I understood that I had a kind master and that a few kind Kurds did exist, even though most of them were terrible. Since that day, I became very fond of him and I stopped stealing. I ate what I was given. I thought that God had put this good man in my path, to teach me to be honest in my work, as well as brave and fearless.

XIV

My master's older brother had four sons and three daughters. Two of his sons were already big fellows; the two youngest were about my age. One was named Hamo and the other, slightly older, was Hajo. The latter was quite stronger than me. As I used to often play with them and as our games usually degenerated into fights, I grew tired of wrestling. They were well-fed and if I had been as well-nourished as them, I could have won on many occasions.

At that time, I found a rusty knife on the ground. I cleaned it and tied it with a rag under my shirt. It was always with me against my body. If I were attacked, I was allowed to defend myself, according to my master's lecture on being brave and fearless.

The heat had arrived. The village well that was close to our house started to dry up. The whole village had to go and fetch water from Daban, the neighboring village. The well there was not so deep but had plenty of water. One day, I was leading my goats to the well across a field. Seated on my donkey with my legs dangling over the sides, I met Hajo, who was also taking his goats to the well. I still do not know what crossed his mind, maybe envy, as he watched me on my donkey while he was on foot. He approached me, pulled roughly on my legs, and flung me to the ground. I bounced back on my feet, as a brave man should do. Immediately, a fight began in the middle of the fields. Nobody was around to separate us. The fellow was big and powerful and he hit me with hard blows I could not match. I was about to lose. I pulled out my secret weapon from under my shirt and held it tight in my hand. I struck back a light blow in the middle of his face and marked it with a long bloody gash. He started to scream and leaving his goats, he ran home crying, "*Aie, Bavo, Bavo, gavouran ess koushteme!*" (Daddy, Daddy, the *giavour* wants to kill me!) Immediately, I threw the stained knife with the rag into the grass, just next to a nest of ants. They rushed out to suck the blood from the blade and their bodies hid the weapon from any inquiring eyes. Then, I led my goats as well as his to the well. Of course, I was scared and was shaking. Shortly after, with his face rudely bandaged, he came back with his older brother. His brother approached me and said, "*Lo erzegherkh!* (You have donkey's nails!) How did you scratch him like that?" And turning towards his younger brother, he said, "*Ghourbaney noney guennem biyo ki du dookhi.*" (You don't deserve the good wheat bread you eat.) And he gave him several blows with a stick he was carrying in his hand. "You are a boy, strong like a donkey, and you let yourself be beat by a *giavour!*" I started to feel slightly reassured. Back home, the boy's parents came immediately to me, seized my hands to check my long fingernails, and said, very surprised, "What nails you have! If you had pulled our son's eye out, we would have killed you!" I went to see my master, trembling with fear, to explain to him the aggression and how I felt compelled to strike back. Of course, I did not give away my secret about the knife. And deep inside, I had doubts about my staying alive after this episode. But just the opposite occurred. My master told me, "*Aferim* (Bravo), in your life, fight as much as you can, but do not let anyone beat you." I was highly surprised that my master was pleased with me. He was proud I had beaten an opponent stronger than me. The boy kept the bandage on his face for a long time and nobody ever found out how I had overcome him and won.

XV

One night, I was deep asleep in my little corner by the door, buried in the straw up to my waist, the top of my body barely protected. Suddenly, I heard my name being called. "Azo, Azo!" I woke up and pricked up my ears, telling myself, "It's certainly my master who has just called me." When he would decide to plow at daybreak, it was not unusual for him to send me to feed the animals in the middle of the night. I was listening carefully, thinking he might call me again. But there was nothing, everything was silent. I then heard a soft voice, very close to me: "Pray the Lord, pray the Lord. How long are you going to suffer like this? This is the very moment to pray to be saved from all this misery." I got up on my knees and started to pray in Kurdish opening my arms wide, "Khodeo, Khodeo (My God, my God). Help me out of my suffering. Do not let me endure this much longer." And I went back to sleep.

When I awakened in the morning, I wondered what had happened. Was it a dream or did I really hear the very soft voice? Whatever it was, I was happy. From the bottom of my heart, I felt that a joyous event had occurred. But what?

My master called and asked me to bring him some water to perform his daily ablutions. I ran to fill up a jug. When I approached him, he was already squatting on his heels and as I poured water in his hands, with large gestures he splashed his face and neck chanting, "*Ya ilaha illallah.*" When it was over, he stood up and looked at me with a startled expression on his face. "What happened to you? You have changed – your face is not the same. You look exactly like a *giavour*. You are not the same Azo!"

I answered that I really did not understand what he meant and I quickly withdrew. My master was thus giving me evidence that it was not a dream and that I had truly been visited during the night. I felt deeply rejoiced!

Days and weeks went by. One morning, a Kurd from the village caught up with me and said, "Azo, listen to me! I'm going to tell you good news, but do not tell your master that I was the one to inform you. Here it is: Many *giavours* are gathered and reunited in the orphanage of Urfa. There, they are taken care of and sent to school. If you can, run away and go over there." I pretended I was not interested because I did not trust him enough and showing my happiness could be used against me. However, I felt that my vision was becoming fulfilled, that the Lord had heard my prayer, and He was not abandoning me.

For some time, I had seen Kurds coming en masse from the Turkish-Russian front to our village. They would then disperse in the neighboring counties. A woman with her two children stayed. She was telling me, "Antranig, Antranig, he is coming with his men." I knew that Antranig was an Armenian name, but as I thought all the Armenians had been slaughtered, I could not believe her. Later on, I understood that on the Caucasian front, the troops of General Antranig were moving forward, which explained the panicked retreat of the Kurds from that region. Now, my master was telling me, "Azo, if by chance the *giavours* came here, you would not let them kill us, would you?" He was really relying upon my good influence to protect him and his family. And I was impatiently waiting, too. Alas! Antranig's troops never reached our region.

XVI

My master became sick and all the work fell on me thereafter. I was grinding down the grains with my feet. I crushed the straw, perched on top of a type of ledge, as was the custom in the country. Suddenly, an ox – a very disobedient one – refused to work any longer, because of the heat and the mean flies which were harassing it. It moved so far away from the boundary I had marked, and I had such a hard time controlling him, that my eyes filled up with tears. It was almost noon and here came Guley, the master's daughter, asking me to take a break and have some lunch. Right away, I freed my two animals who dashed away like crazy towards a corn field. They were in search of a cool spot and eager to get rid of the flies. The owner of the field was yelling, wondering whose animals they were. I was ready to interfere, and was about to place myself in front of them, when my mistress arrived. In a swift move, she led them back to the path. But the oxen, so exhausted and tormented by thirst, walked across the fields. They went in the direction of water, to the village of Daban. I managed to catch up and lead them to the well. On my way, I looked for my knife, which I had tossed away the day I had struggled with Hajo. I found it and wrapped it around my waist with the rag, which was not far away.

I was a few minutes away from the well when my mistress – hustling and even running – caught up with me. She, in a very nasty mood and driven by anger, ordered, "Take off all your clothes, you filthy *giavour!*" First, I thought it was a joke, but she meant what she said. So I slowly scratched myself, loosening the rag and letting the knife fall with the shirt on top of it – so it would not be noticed. She grabbed it with the knife and the rag still inside. She bundled my measly belongings, including my cap, and walked to the well – leaving me all alone, as naked as the day I was born. I realized then, she was taking advantage of her husband's sickness to get rid of me.

I hid on the side of the road, ashamed and hopeless. Where could I go? What should I do? It was impossible to reveal myself. If only I had my shirt! I then came up with a plan. I would wait here for her return. She would be carrying her goatskin full of water on her shoulders with my clothes on top. I would jump on her, grab my shirt, and run.

However, I kept on worrying, "If I don't succeed, what will happen to me? Who will take me in for the night?" At that moment, I saw an old lady from our village coming my way. I knew her. She had tied a rope around her calf's neck to go to the well. She had a short, wide, and stubby body which provided a good shelter. Besides, she had very bad eyesight. As soon as she reached my hiding place, I came out without being noticed and walked behind the calf. The animal became frightened and started to move from left to right. The old lady turned her head to see what was happening. "Don't worry Mrs. Ansha, it's Azo, I'm also going to the well." She gave a quick glance in my direction and did not notice my extreme nudity. I kept on walking, patting the calf, who then calmed down.

Just as we were reaching the well, I saw my bundle of rags set by the side of the road away from the animals' path. At this time of day, the villagers were crowding around the well. It was my mistress's turn to pull out her water and she could not let go of the rope. I seized the opportunity, quickly grabbing my shirt (luckily with its contents) and fled! She started squealing and screaming, attacking my father's beard, which at that time, was a serious insult. People around the well yelled with her, not knowing why. I was already far away and managed to put my shirt back on. As for the knife, it was still there but I did not want to keep it any longer. I thought it had somehow played a part in my leaving. I threw it in a hole and covered it up. My fate was now in the hands of God. I took a deep breath. Some time later, I saw my mistress leave the well and go back home. As I expected, she was carrying her goatskin full of water on her back. I then walked to the well calmly and drank some cool water. I was tired and upset. Two boys my age were still on the premises and I came closer to them, hoping to get their opinion about the incident. But I quickly felt their hostility and feared they could take my shirt, which I had such a hard time recovering. I had spent three years at my second master's home.

XVII

Here I was in Daban, alone by the well and feeling lost. I had neither a master nor shelter. What else could I do but find a new one? If I stayed outside, I would certainly be killed during the night. I looked around hoping to find a new, welcoming home. In the distance, I saw an old overweight lady working around her house. She was coming and going, in and out, in slow motions. I was reassured by her age and her gait. I had to find a place for the night, as I was so weak due to emotions, exhaustion and hunger. I walked forward.

I met the lady face to face on her doorstep. I begged for a slice of bread. She looked at me, asked a few questions, and rapidly guessed my whole situation, origin, and condition. In my own words, I told the story of my misfortune, avoiding all gossip that could hurt my previous master, who I cared for. As I was describing my miserable fate, the sickness of my master, and my disgrace, she kept on looking at me with kindness. In turn, she told me she had recently become a widow and was living with her son. In fact, she was in need of someone to keep her goats.

I ate well that night and met her son, who was in his twenties. It was my first day at my third master's home. The following day, I left for the pasture grounds with about thirty goats, which was quite a comfortable number for village people to own. After a few days, my young master asked me to work with him. The goats would be taken over by someone else. The harvest had been collected and the wheat was ready to be ground. I was given the task of separating the straw from the ears and sieving the grains.

My young master and his mother were watching me, amazed. I was working with enthusiasm, doing such a good job, and showing the full range of my strength. I was well-fed and well-treated. My young master was praising me openly in front of everybody.

In the crowd, there was a man responsible for checking the field work and the produce of the harvest. He was a kind of manager for big property owners. He looked strong and important with his gun at his waist. This man had watched me work and had listened to my master's praises. He approached me and greeted me, "*Merhabo*" (hello) and I replied, "*Merhabo.*" He sat on a heap of straw and had me sit in front of him. He asked jokingly if I would follow him to his country. "Where is your country?" I asked with a certain curiosity, because my deepest wish was to return to a big city, similar to the one where I was born. In my heart, I had set my hopes on meeting my fellow countrymen to speak my native tongue, share my suffering, and maybe learn news of my family. "Five hours from here," he answered and gave me the name of a village unknown to me. "No!" I replied without faltering, "I don't want to go." He tried to force me to go and to ask my master for permission to leave. He was confident he could get a favorable answer through intimidation. "I won't ask," I said. He became brutal and grew into a rage. "I will take you by force." "I will run away!" "Aha, you will run away," he said pointing to his gun. "I'm not scared of it." "You are not scared! You, dirty *giavour* – here, this is for you!'" He pulled out his gun and fired. I felt like a warm rush of air on my arm but I could not fathom what was happening. It had to be a firecracker like the ones kids played with. However, I saw my master run up to me and his mother followed, moving as fast as she could. My master placed himself between my aggressor and myself and ordered him to leave. Meanwhile, other people had gathered around us. They had all understood it was not a game.

It was serious, but since I had not been hurt, they remained silent. Facing me, the stout Kurd kept on threatening me with his gun. I knew that if the first bullet had missed me, the second one would not. My mistress finally arrived, grabbed my hand, and walked away with me. The next day, I was sent back to my goats to protect me from any other incidents.

My previous mistress had heard about the attack and was disappointed I had not been shot. She claimed that if she could catch me, she would throw me into the well with no chance of return and with guaranteed death. I even saw her one night wandering around the house. I hid in the dark and felt threatened from every direction. I decided it was time to flee.

The next morning, while I was leading my goats, I met a young lad I knew well and asked him to keep them while I went to the next village on important business. I would be right back. He refused and remained adamant for days. Finally, I presented my hidden knife, which he took, agreeing to help the following morning. I left him my goats, knowinghe would take them back to my master at dusk if I was not back. I left the village, never to return, after having spent ten days with my third master.

I had a whole day ahead of me to find a new master before dark. Where to go? Where to stay? How to find a master rich enough to provide me with decent meals? I was wandering aimlessly, crossing two to three villages, anxious to get as far as possible from my enemies. Finally, I reached Bozdepe, which I knew from riding my donkey there to get some barley for my second master. I walked to the well to quench my thirst, but also to collect some information. The well was the best place to meet people and start conversations. I hoped to find my fourth master by lingering there. After a while, some women arrived carrying their buckets and pitchers. I started to talk to them and tell them my story. By chance, one of them knew my second master quite well and how mean-spirited his wife was. She agreed to take me with her. In spite of my weariness, I carried her bucket of water. I was delighted that someone was willing to give me shelter for the night. She appeared friendly and I thought she might find me a place to work in the village if she did not want me to stay. When we arrived at her home, she declared she had decided to keep me.

XVIII

This woman, whom I called *Khatoon* (great lady), became my fourth master. She had several children. Her husband was enrolled as a soldier and was on leave twice a year.

My work consisted of doing some housecleaning, getting water at the well, and mainly looking after the children. I was not an expert at cleaning, but I knew all about children. In fact, I had babysat Ibrahim Bekir's last child from his birth up to my departure. This little boy had tantrums as soon as he would see me and I was like his toy. When I returned home after my day of work, I had to carry him on my back. I would then walk, run, or romp with him so he would not cry. I was his *ishoog* (donkey). I was often tired of this chore and I would pinch him in a sneaky way. He would then stop climbing on my back for some time – to his parents' surprise! I knew how to get along with children and in this new home, I had plenty of time, since I had no other task to perform. Sometimes, I had three or four children hanging on my body and I would walk on all fours with them. Once in a while, I would tumble down with them to make them laugh or because I was jealous of their happiness. I would also carry them one at a time, on my shoulders, all around the house for a private walk. I had to be the beast of burden to earn my food. Often my eyes would fill up with tears because their screams of joy would remind me of my brothers and sisters, my friends, my house with its garden and two swimming pools. I was no longer the spoiled baby brother and I had a hard time accepting the role of clown. I would dry my tears with my filthy hands and save them for a better opportunity.

In fact, the work was not tiring. While I was entertaining the children, my mistress was chatting left and right with her neighbors. During her absence, the children had the habit of eating treats they had secretly and very skillfully snatched. I did the same. However, as I realized my dirty hands could betray me, I used all kinds of tricks to grab the cookies. I must admit that since the beginning of my captivity, it had been the first chance I had to taste these sugary delights and it brought me great joy.

I had an instinctive fear of soldiers and I was dreading her husband's return. "Who knows," I told myself, "he may be murdering my brothers at this very moment. If he comes back, he may kill me!" These thoughts were troubling me and a deep-seated anxiety disturbed my present comfort and happiness. Two weeks later, my mistress asked me if I was willing to go to her brother's, who needed me. I could not refuse. This man was living in the same village, just a few houses over. He became my new master.

XIX

My fifth master was Khatoon's brother, a man I already knew and who also knew me. He was the man I was sent to by my second master, to get some extra barley during the shortage. I had not reached the village of Bozdepe by luck. I had dreamed of meeting someone I knew and my hope had been fulfilled. I wanted to be taken in by a kind master, who was very young or very old, someone weak, or a woman. I feared the overpowering, strict masters who would threaten me when my intention was to leave.

My new master appeared friendly. He owned fields, vineyards, and a garden. My job consisted of farming cultures I did not know, since I came from much deprived regions. I was happy to learn new things and I worked earnestly for two months, until he told me,

"You must return to Mederbaz, to Ibrahim Bekir's. I was told he has recovered. He needs you and is looking for you." "My master Ibrahim Bekir! But I thought he was dead," I said. "Allah! Allah! He is alive and all sick people do not die!" he replied. I immediately added, "Allah! Allah!" wondering why I was told he was dead. He brought up the subject many times. In the village, people started to comment. They even uttered threatening words against me. "If you do not return to your master and if you do not apologize, he will find you, wherever you are and kill you!" I became frightened. During his illness, his wife had persecuted me and had even tried to have me killed. That was why I had fled. Now that he was getting better, he was asking for me. I was fearing the worst. It could be a trap – his wife's strategy to get back at me and have me murdered. What should I do? To go or not to go? I wanted to know the truth. I wanted to talk to him but I suspected his wife of manipulation. Then I remembered my master's strong words, "Be brave and fearless throughout your life!" Why should I be scared? I made up my mind to see him and tell him the whole truth.

Thus, one evening, I warned my fifth master I would be leaving by daylight the next morning. I took the road back to Mederbaz, walking fast to reach the well of Daban before noon, which I did after a five-hour walk. As usual, at this hour of the day, the place was crowded with people and animals. I expected to meet someone from Mederbaz to collect information about my master, but still feared meeting his terrible wife. I walked forward and discreetly made my way through the bustle, where I finally recognized a village dweller. "Is it true that my master is looking for me?" I asked. "The poor man, he is so sick he often does not know who he is," he answered. This information calmed me but I wanted to know more. Why was I summoned to come back? What was the scheme behind all this? I noticed Guley and I called her cheerfully but with some caution:

"Do you recognize me?"

"Yes," she said with an upset look on her girlish little face.

"What are you doing here? Why did you come?" she quickly added.

"I am inquiring about your daddy's health."

"He is still lying down on his bed sick."

"Does he sometimes ask about me?"

"Who do you think you are? He does not talk to anyone – not even to us. Why do you think he should care about you, you dirty *giavour*?" I was saddened by her last words because she was dear to me. For her, I had played the *ishoog* (donkey) but I was relieved to learn that my master was not looking for me. All this was his cruel wife's secret plot. I left the premises – or more precisely, I ran away, leaving Guley behind me in a state of surprise.

I did not need to be frightened any longer by my worst enemy. I knew the truth and I had discovered her scheme. It was past lunchtime and my stomach was making strange noises. I was exhausted and hungry. What should I do? I had no strength left and my legs could barely carry me. Was this weakness only due to hunger? Or was it because of the memory of my good old master and my return to the well? Once more, I was left alone, homeless, and without a master. I could not even go back to my third master, whose goats I had abandoned to go to Bozdepe.

Starving and emotionally exhausted, I slowly moved to the other side of the village of Daban. I saw a house where the door was in poor shape. I knocked and someone yelled back to come in. An old man was lying on a mattress set on the floor. I said, "*Apo, Apo, Pariecki non mede khera bavettde.*" (Give me a piece of bread in honor of your father.) The man raised a dirty face with sharp-looking eyes. I felt secure in the presence of this weak old man, who certainly would not mistreat me. He asked me to close the door.

"*Lo dou koure keyi?*" (Who are you the son of?)

"*Koure tekhdegkinem.*" (I am the son of no one.)

"*Dou gavour lo?*" (You are a *giavour*?)

"*Elhamdoullah ez musulmanem.*" (I am a Muslim.)

He observed me and I could tell he knew I was a *giavour* and he knew all about my past. He asked, "Would you like to stay with us?" "Why not?" I answered. I then confessed I had left my master back in Mederbaz because of his wife who threatened to throw me into the well or strangle me. I was terrified. The old man said, "*Lo*, look at me. Neither your master, nor his wife, nor even a pasha have any rights upon you. You are neither their son nor their parent – even less their slave. You should not be afraid and you must never be afraid. You must grow up with no fear and go through life fearless." These strong words invigorated me. He then stood up, gave me some bread with yogurt, and added, "Eat and pray to God. You were hungry and now you have food to eat. Thank God for all of this."

I decided to stay with him, not only for the food, but mainly for his encouraging words. I was looking for a kind master like Ibrahim Bekir.

XX

His wife, who was old and childless, became attached to me and fed me with generosity. I was less tense, my life was becoming comfortable, and I was gaining strength. After several days, my master wondered if I knew how to sow corn. I answered that I did. I remembered I had learned this skill with my second master, after being beaten and pricked a great deal. He then called upon his young neighbor who was always willing to help. He asked him to have the plow repaired at Asman, the next village, as soon as possible. The following day, the young man left with the plow, as was planned. My master was inside, lying down sick. His wife was busy preparing the daily bread in a shed near the house. All of a sudden, I heard a voice coming from inside me, telling me, "Your place is not here. You must go on and join other Armenian orphans – and maybe find members of your family." An incredible energy rushed inside me. I had to take advantage of the situation. Nobody was watching over me and I belonged to no one. I decided to prepare my escape. I went to see the old lady in the shed and very politely asked for a hot biscuit. I started to eat right away – then a second – and a third. I did not dare ask for more. I was rested and fed, so the time was right to flee. I checked all around and left the village very carefully. As soon as I was away on the road, I sped up my pace and started running, feeling free, free at last. No one had any right to chase me.

I walked a long time and without stopping, passed by Bozdepe where I had just been a few days earlier. I proceeded on the road, when a horseman arrived behind me. I was free, I should not be scared, I did not owe anything to anyone. I slowed down my pace and let the horseman approach. He recognized me and I knew that he was from Bozdepe. We exchanged a few words of welcome and I asked where he was heading. He said Urfa, this large city where Armenian orphans like me were gathered. I immediately retorted, "Me too, I am going to Urfa." It was my deepest wish, my most cherished hope. I did not know how to get there so I asked, "Is it still far?" "A good eighteen to twenty-hour walk." I thought it was much too far and it had to be done in several stages. I also wondered what would happen to me in Urfa. I had no idea. While walking, I was reflecting upon it and a feeling of despair came over me. I expected some help from the horseman, a little support – maybe a ride on his horse with him. He did not make the slightest attempt to assist me. Why? Was I still a *giavour* in his eyes? Wasn't I a Muslim? After an hour – he on his horse and I on foot – we arrived near Aghmughara. It was the very village where I had found my dearest mom lying dead next to me. It was the very village where the Kurd threw her body in a hole unprotected from dogs and jackal attacks. My body started shaking, remembering all the suffering, and my feet were glued to the ground. I knew I had to stop in the village. Besides, everybody would certainly recognize me there. I told the horseman I was going to the village and we went our separate ways. I lost sight of him after a while and I remained at the same place, unable to move, prostrate with grief. I waited until I recovered some of my strength and spirit.

I noticed a tent not too far off and decided to head towards it very slowly. I asked for some water. I quenched my thirst and cleaned my face. The lady of the tent was watching me and as soon as I had finished refreshing myself she said, "Aren't you the boy who stayed with Ibrahim Bekir?" She asked many more questions, which I answered in the most evasive possible way. Soon after, a Kurd I recognized as being one of the rich dwellers of the village arrived. He also recognized me and instantly greeted me, "*O, merhabo,* Aziz!" He asked me what I was doing and before I had the time to answer, he grabbed my arm and led me to his home. He introduced me to his wife called *Khatoon* (great lady) and declared, "You will stay with us. You will eat butter, cheese, yogurt, and cream. This winter we will take you to Mesopotamia." With these words, he cut a large slice of bread and generously spread it with butter. I devoured it without missing one crumb. But I was a little confused. I did not know what to do any longer. I had left with the firm intention to join my people and now I was hesitating. Should I stay or should I leave? In fact, the taste of the good bread decided it all, and I made up my mind to stay.

XXI

My seventh master's name was Ramo Khelkhalli. There were four brothers in the village but since one had died, Ramo married the deceased one's wife – which was according to their custom. She had two infant daughters. The eldest brother had two sons in their twenties. All these men were excellent horsemen and always carried weapons. The three brothers owned large farmland, and a good hundred sheep with some camels.

On my very first night, I was sent to work to replace a shepherd who had just left. I was given a large thick wool coat to use both as a garment, as well as a mattress or bed. It was the first time in my whole life I had to keep sheep at night. It was so hot during the day that the animals could not feed themselves correctly, whereas in the cool of the night, they grazed peacefully and abundantly. The brothers' herds were mixed, so I left the village at sunset with a professional shepherd. He was a Kurd, who had fought on the Russian battlefront. We drove the sheep to pasture, heading towards the slope of the neighboring mountain. So there I was, the big heavy coat on my back, walking barefoot in the darkening evening, towards an unknown place behind a large flock of sheep. The night fell rapidly and I could barely see in front of me – only the length of my shadow. I stepped on rocks, thorns, and rough plants – and I cried most of the way, because my feet were in such terrible pain. We finally reached the pasture. We were each standing at opposite ends of the herd, but it was so large we could not see – only hear – each other. In case of wolf attacks, I was supposed to scream, *"Houal! Houal!"* Since there were no weapons or dogs for protection, we had to rely upon ourselves exclusively. In the deep night, wolves did attack. My sheep left at once. I could hear the sound of their galloping, as they desperately ran away, but

I could not see a thing. It seemed like the wind had swept them away. I was shell-shocked, so panicked, that my tongue became paralyzed in my mouth. I could not speak, nor scream, nor utter the slightest sound. I was the victim of an overpowering fear. Where were my sheep? Where was my companion? I started crying. All the promises of butter, cream, and yogurt were a lure. I was only a child lost in the heart of the night. Finally, I heard the far away call of my companion but I could not answer. He was yelling, "Where are you? Speak, you fool, dumb idiot!" and many more irreverent expressions and profanities. He was coming closer and his presence slowly unravelled my anxiety. He saw me and was so enraged, he was about to hit me, when I managed to explain my state of panic and despair. He laughed and made fun of me. For him, it was nothing. He told me the sheep had sensed danger, and had gathered so tightly in a compact group, that none of them could be pulled apart. It was an instinctive strategy of defense and they were used to doing so. The wolves had missed their attack. He advised me to let the sheep stay together so they could sleep. I followed all his recommendations precisely. We stayed close to them and made ourselves ready for some rest. The following day before noon, we arrived at the village and after napping a few hours, we returned to the mountain. This is the life of a shepherd, sleeping off and on, a few hours a day, a few hours at night.

I told my master how hard the job seemed to me, and how painful it was to walk barefoot on stony paths in the dark. He promised to buy me some short boots. He tried his best to comfort me, saying he was expecting a real shepherd soon. He also added that he would talk to his brother's shepherd, and make the situation more bearable for me.

A few nights later, we were on the mountain with several shepherds and among us was one of my master's brother's sons. Sleeping by the sheep was thus out of the question, and we had to be on the watch all night long. So here were gathered hundreds and hundreds of sheep, a much larger number than usual. I felt less frightened, even though the distance between each of us was still important. I could not make them out, but sometimes I would hear the signal, "*Ho, ho, ho, dah, dah, chahre.*" These words were addressed to the sheep. They felt protected, that men were watching over them. These words were also addressed to the other shepherds, to evaluate the distance between them. To men and animals, these were words of comfort.

I could notice from the direction of the voices that the shepherds had gathered to chat. I was all alone in the dead of night, far from them all. It was my turn to watch and everything seemed under control. The grass was generous where we were, and the sheep were grazing peacefully. I decided to sit for a while and yelled the usual signal, "*Ho, ho, ho . . .*" Slowly, I slid to the ground feeling drowsy, and was soon overcome by sleep.

All of a sudden, I opened my eyes: I was completely alone. I could not smell the animals, nor could I hear the sound of the sheep, nor the echo of human voices. I did not know how long I had slept but it was still pitch dark. I ran blindly to the top of the mountain, and there I howled the name of the shepherd I knew, "Messo, lo, lo, Messo!" I repeated it several times. Silence. I cried and yelled and cried. No answer. My voice should have been carried far away in the night! They must have moved quite far. I thought about going down to the village, but I did not know where I was or how to orient myself. It was so dark, I decided to sit down. I then buried my head in my coat-mattress, numbed with fear. But I felt under my body a strange little noise, like a constant scratching. I realized I had settled myself on the hole of a mole or a rodent, digging its tunnels under me. I thought, "What is that poor little animal doing in this deserted land, far from everything? What solitude, even deeper than mine, is it living in?" I changed my place and the noise stopped. I looked all around and I still did not see anything. I worried about what wolves or jackals would do to me if they found me. I thus set my head on a rock, curled myself up in my coat – protecting my hands, feet, and head – and finally fell into a deep sleep. Suddenly, I woke up feeling a heavy weight pressing on my body. I wondered what it could be before I realized it was the heat of the sun, already high in the sky. How happy and relieved I felt! I quickly jumped to my feet and looked all around. Still, no one in sight. I ran to the other side of the mountain – back and forth – and finally noticed them. They were all gathered together. They started laughing aloud when I appeared in front of them, my face marked with anxiety. I was a real beginner! It did happen to me several more times, with no harm involved. My master finally hired a real shepherd. He was short, stout and friendly-looking, with a large smile on his face. His name was Cheko and had been a shepherd for fifteen years. He had a year-long contract with my master and was paid. He soon became my friend.

XXII

A quite well-off Kurdish family arrived in our village. They brought with them an Armenian orphan about my age. We became friends on the first day. He was good-natured and more intelligent than Hamed Ali, the other Armenian orphan in the village, who strongly denied his origin, his language, and his past. "I am a Muslim," he kept repeating, while looking away. My new friendship brought great comfort to me. In secret, hiding from everybody, we would speak Armenian, even if we destroyed our dear mother tongue. We felt great joy, realizing we had not completely forgotten the language of our childhood, and the love for our country. But to our great sorrow, this happiness did not last long.

The winter was approaching and my master got ready to move to Mesopotamia, as he did every single year. There, the animals would have plenty of grass. Many families coming from different villages, including Bozdepe, traveled together to reinforce the security of the caravan, in case of aggression or danger. I was excited to leave and the name of Mesopotamia was dreamlike to me. I would see new places, I would meet new people, maybe get closer to a big city, and find a better host family. Furthermore, Mesopotamia was a place where I could hide if I ever decided to escape. My heart was full of hope.

The day before the departure, I did not forget to pay a visit to my new friend's family. I said goodbye to each of them and at the end, the master confessed he had known me for some time – about three years. I had just been adopted by Ibrahim Bekir. He had wanted to buy me, but my second master had refused. He had then decided to adopt another orphan with whom he was very happy, adding, "Armenians are good labor for us." What a pity, I thought! I would have lived a better life with him and not suffered as much. I said goodbye and noticed tears filling up in my friend's eyes. He was saddened by my departure, and I could tell he would have loved to come along.

The following day, we loaded the camels with tents and all the necessary equipment for the journey and the stay. We formed a caravan: the children and women were perched on the camels and had the best places; then, the men on horseback, grouped together and heavily armed; and the last ones on foot, like me, holding long sticks to guide the camels – who were moving quite freely and widely apart from one another. The shepherds knew the road well. They had left ahead of us at daybreak. Finally, our turn came to leave the village.

After several days of travel through mountains, valleys, and plains, we reached Mesopotamia. I had dreamed of arriving near a big city; I had dreamed of meeting new people; I had dreamed of eventually running away – and my deception was immense. We could see neither villages nor houses, just rolling hills covered here and there with ruins of ancient human dwellings. The grass was dried out, and some thin shrubs covered with thorns were trying to grow along with thistles. However, this desolate landscape turned out to be a camel's delight.

Up to now, I had walked barefoot and I hurt so much that I could not stop crying. The camels, suffering from their excessive loads, were struggling along the rocky roads. Their hoofs would roll on stones or be caught in unexpected ditches. I would call for help just in time to prevent any accident or mutilation. I was exhausted from fatigue and pain.

Finally, we established our first caravan settlement. My master and some of his fellows left with a few camels to get some material and food. They came back a few days later with, to my great joy, a pair of short boots! I had expected them for so long – since the very day my master had promised them. A strong emotion filled my heart at the sight of the boots. I saw my family, my home, where I had all I needed. These shoes brought back happy memories and I could not hide my excitement! With my new boots on and a long stick in my hand, I became everybody's camel driver from now on, leading a herd of twenty animals. We did not stay too long at the same place – maybe ten to fifteen days at the most. We were always in search of better pastures, where the grass would be taller and more abundant. We finally reached a place where several tents were already gathered, forming a small village. "Who are these people? Are they Kurds?" I asked my master. "No, they are Arabs and they belong to the Eneza tribe. They are not nomads like us; they live on these premises.

This is their country. They are at home here with their camels in this immense, remote open space." We settled our caravan not far from them, with our tents grouped together.

The following day, at the head of my herd of camels, I left the campsite for the whole day. I thought of myself a true camel driver with all the experience I had gained from the journey. I was even allowed to climb on their backs to shout orders to them. However, I was facing a real problem trying to discipline them. I had to get down and run left and right to keep them together. It was exhausting. On the opposite side of the hill, however, I observed a hundred camels grazing peacefully without getting scattered. At sunset, the Arab shepherd climbed on one camel, set himself in front, and all the others followed him in an obedient line. He was yelling, "*Ho holov, ho, holov!*" It was the signal given to return home, down to the tent village. The animals gathered willingly in an uninterrupted chain so long that the shepherd could not see the end. It was like a mile-long wave moving in and out of the hill. The shepherd was not showing any sign of anxiety or concern. He knew his camels were soothed by his presence and lulled by his chant, echoing in the valley.

From where I was, I watched this perfect communion between man and animals with admiration. As for me, I barely managed to gather my little disobedient flock. Now that I had heard and memorized the chant, I decided to apply it to my camels. I climbed on the back of the oldest one and started yelling and singing the way I had witnessed. I took the lead and walked slowly away. To my surprise, no one followed. On the contrary, my camels were moving further apart. Here I was again, forced to jump down and run after each of them, screaming, yelling, hitting them with my stick to pull them together. I finally succeeded, and was impatient to get back to my tent to swallow my ration of soup, which I so deserved. I was exhausted from running all day between these restless camels.

The next evening, on my return, a camel was missing. He had become mad and it had been impossible to bring him back. The more I ran after him, the more he ran away. I warned the animal's owner and told him about my desperate efforts. He jumped on a horse at once, and left like a gust of wind, disappearing into the dust. He returned two days later, walking side by side with his camel. It took him that long to find the animal and bring him back. What had happened? Indeed, the camel had become crazy and even his master had a hard time approaching him. He had waited for the animal to calm down by following him from far away, without being noticed, so his feeling of freedom would remain intact. In fact, the owner had not been luckier than me! Remembering the shepherd from the other side of the hill, I thought the time was right to go and talk to my master. I explained the whole story to him and asked why I could not gather my camels the way it miraculously happened with the Arab camel driver. Was there a secret I should be aware of? My master was sitting in the back of his tent on a thick woolen carpet and looked extremely calm. He wore a big beard and thick mustache, and I could detect a kind of sneer piercing through his mass of hairs. He knew I was both worried and irritated. He took the time to rub and stroke his long beard before giving his final statement. "Calm down, you won't be a camel driver for much longer. We are going to hire an Arab shepherd and you will take care of the lambs. You see, our camels will never come close to being as obedient as the Arab ones. Each of our camels comes from a different region: One from Urfa, one from Suruj, another one from Birejik. They share no bond in common and never will. On the other hand, these hundred Arab camels were born here, they know one another well, they grew up together, they are from this land. If one of these camels is sold to go somewhere else, he himself will turn wild and unruly like ours."

This explanation suited me well and I said to myself that what applied to camels could also be applied to men: We all carry within our hearts the love of our homeland and of our kin. Among the Kurdish people, I, Azo, was a misfit.

XXIII

All day long, the camels were grazing on bushes whose stems abounded with a liquid similar to milk, called *geyvourouh*. It was a rich nutrient and the animals quickly became stronger and heavier. They also turned more rebellious and could, on occasion, be aggressive. I remember seeing them blowing like turkeys, belching noisily, and spitting chunks of red-looking flesh. They were hideous and their sight frightened me. Several times, during our journey, my mistress pointed to graves of men who had died because of mad camels. For all those reasons, during that period, I approached them with great caution and threw stones to gather them.

At last, the Arab camel driver arrived. He replaced me, and I felt relieved to give up such strenuous work. I returned to being a shepherd with Cheko. The lamb births were increasing in number. I would look after them and take them out daily for a few hours. Some had already started to graze, and the younger ones seemed to watch them so they could learn. The work was giving us lots of trouble, mainly when we had to change campsites. I was no longer in the caravan and I was glad about it, because Cheko and I got along like brothers. Of course, the task was hard, especially when the births multiplied, but I was rewarded by his friendship. It sometimes happened that several lambs were born at the same time. We would carry three or four in our arms, and after half an hour, release them to let them walk

Birejik and its ancient citadel.

by their mothers. Then, another load of births would be waiting for us, and we had to start all over again.

We were underfed and all day we had to move our flock from one hill to another with empty stomachs. As we were starving, Cheko would catch an ewe, turn it on its back and we would each take turns sucking the milk. Our bellies would swell, but our hunger would soon come back with a rage; since the food was light, we had to resort to this strategy quite often. Cheko confessed that in fifteen years, he had never seen such a stingy master. Where he worked before, the food was plentiful with leftovers after each meal. I was drooling just listening to him, and I wondered why I had never met such a generous master. I hoped one day Cheko would find me a good one, far away from this master; I had willingly accepted to live with him because of his promise of butter, yogurt, and cream, which were terribly wanting.

To tell the truth, my master was not as miserly as his wife; in fact, he really dreaded her, which was a rare flaw among Kurdish men. We sometimes used to see them fight. The woman would take her hair band (which crowned her head to hold her veil) and slide it around his neck. She would squeeze it to a point of strangulation screaming, "Idiot! Worthless! You don't even measure up to your brother's nail!" My master, who had loved his brother dearly and had married his widow according to the custom, suffered this martyrdom with patience and respect. However, he had been unfortunate to have married a violent shrew. Cheko and I often interfered to separate them and save our master from his spouse's terrible blows.

I did hope that these fights we were witnessing and breaking up would bring us a type of reward, but our daily share remained unchanged: two small loaves of bread each. "You will see what I will do from now on!" I told Cheko. And I started stealing all I could.

My mistress liked me somewhat, because I was useful to her and to her daughters, who always stayed inside the tent. She often called me to scratch her girls' backs, which were covered with pimples and boils. I did it to make myself agreeable, and my hands and nails were covered with their blood. They screamed and asked for more. Near their beds I had discovered a food storage, and I took advantage of my position to withdraw all I could. All this was very disgusting, knowing that the girls, as well as their mother, were contaminated by leprosy. But it was the least of my concerns. They were even surprised that I did not catch the disease, saying, "You belong to the race of goats while we are of sheep, and goats don't catch sheep diseases." I used to laugh, having only one obsession in mind, to satiate my hunger.

At night, lying down in the dark in the immense tent, I planned schemes for stealing. My bed was set behind a kind of bamboo screen, on the other side of my mistress. A little further away, the camels and the horse were tied up for the night. I can still recall the smell of the animals, and hear their sounds of sneezing, scratching, or lamenting. I had noticed a storage of raisins next to my mistress's couch near her head. One night, when everybody was fast asleep, I stood up, opened the bag, and carefully filled up one of my boots – since I did not have any pockets. I put everything back and went to see Cheko with my plunder. He was both surprised and delighted. He thought I was smart. He filled up his pockets and gave back my boot. "From now on, we have to steal whenever we can," I told him. I was proud of my achievement and decided not to give it up!

Another night, we had just gone to bed and Khatoon was getting drowsy. Outside, the sky was dark, swept by a violent snowstorm. No one could see further than a few yards. Cheko, who was left all alone in the frightening night, had already gathered the sheep near the tent. He came in to ask for instructions, "What should I do in this weather? Should I bring the sheep in or stay outside?" He was standing next to a large bag full of dried, lean portions of cheese – called *chortan* – which we used to put in our soups during the winter. While talking to our mistress, he calmly filled up his pockets with entire impunity, under the protection of the pitch darkness. When Khatoon replied that she preferred to have the sheep stay outside because of the risk of incidents with the camels and the horse – he left. The next day – and for three days in a row – we ate cheese to our fill, with Cheko repeating how smart he was, too.

One morning, I was sitting next to Khatoon, in front of the fire. In the frying pan, a large chunk of butter was melting and I had my eye on it. How to get to it? Suddenly, Cheko rushed inside. Just as Khatoon turned her head, I seized the opportunity, grabbed the unmelted butter with my fingers, and stuffed it in my mouth. Cheko, who was watching me, started to blush, shake, and stutter. Some time after, when we were alone, he confessed, "I didn't know you were that daring! I was fearing for you. How did you ever grab that piece of butter without burning your fingers?" Starting that day, we planned our thefts: he would entertain Khatoon while I would steal at my convenience. We had finalized a way to relieve our hunger.

XXIV

The lamb births kept increasing while I was their main shepherd. When we traveled, we mixed them with the sheep. Cheko knew the way through the mountains, but this time the road was long, and we were delayed by the great number of births. Once, when my arms became overloaded, I carried the newborn lambs in a bag on my shoulder. Fortunately, the lambs could walk shortly after birth, but the bag kept filling up. The baby kids were causing me trouble, since they needed more time to get on their feet. We kept some goats among the sheep, which were useful to the herd. On torrid days during the summer, the sheep – who suffered from the heat because of their thick fleece – grazed peacefully under the shade of goats. During the winter, however, the goats – who were susceptible to the cold – were able to graze, while being protected by the warmth of the sheep. The more lively and frisky goats headed the herd, and when a wolf would grab one of them, they would make a hoarse sound – immediately warning the shepherd. When wolves carried away sheep, they would not make a sound. Sheep and goats, due to their natural exchange of favors, lived in harmony within the herd.

One evening, many kids were born in the mountains. We had to slow down our course, and were unable to reach the caravan, which was too far from us. The night was falling and Cheko was scared. "If the Arab looters find out where we are, they will dash down on us in a gang and steal all our newborns," he told me, based on his experience. Fortunately, that very night, we only met Kurds, and the fear of an attack somehow dissipated. By daybreak, we had reached the Arab territory. We left the main path and hid all day with the herd to avoid crossing any Arabs. We finally arrived at our caravan late at night, heavily weighed down with kids, and overwhelmed by fatigue. Our mistress, worried sick and in tears, thought we had been kidnapped with our herds. Her anxiety had increased due to the absence of her husband, who had gone to Urfa. He had left for a few days with all the camels. Under these circumstances and despite her usual harshness, Khatoon made an effort to provide us with larger portions of food, recognizing the supreme effort we had achieved. As for me, I had never been that exhausted. I felt rage and despair, longing for only one thing: to run away from this cursed place.

When my master came back, he gathered his men and reported what he had heard and seen, as he did following each trip. Some time after, Cheko came to see me in secret. He told me he had good news for me, although he had promised the master not to repeat it. He said, "The *Ingiliz* (English) have entered Urfa. All the *giavours* are gathered and placed in orphanages, where they are given clothes, shoes, food, and education. No matter where they are scattered, they will be reunited and treated in the same manner. So imagine, Azo, the large city of Urfa is full of *Ingiliz* soldiers. You must find a way to go there, because here, you are tormented and mistreated. But wait a bit longer. Let the winter go by. Then, we will return home, and from there, you will run away. If you decided to leave now, you would get lost, because it is far and you do not know the way." I was so transported to hear the news, I thought I was dreaming. I immediately thought about my family, with the genuine hope of seeing one of them again. I did not know how to thank Cheko for his friendship and trust. And each time he received new information on the subject, he would share it with me as soon as he could.

XXV

Days and weeks went by. The lambs were growing up. I kept them day and night and had become a true shepherd. At night, some of us used to get together. One evening, as I was standing next to a bush, I decided to make it the border of my pasture, so my lambs would not be scattered. But one of them moved somewhat aside. Although I was keeping a watchful eye on the bush, a bold and clever wolf had managed to stealthily hide in it. I could only see the lamb disappear at once without a cry while the others, terrified, ran away towards the bulk of the herd. It was pitch dark. I turned, stunned and speechless. My friends were calling, "Oh! Oh! What's happening?" "The wolf carried a lamb away!" "You idiot! Run after it!" I could barely see and I was not about to venture by myself on the uneven slope. I moved a few steps forward and told them I could not find it. I was not afraid of wolves anymore, but I just did not want to take such a risk all alone in the dark. In the morning at daybreak, I saw eagles and other birds of prey coming from everywhere. What strange instinct had alerted them to the exact place of the sacrifice! They led us to the spot the wolf had devoured its victim, but its remains did not help to identify it. Back to the herd, we had to separate the lambs and count them. None of mine were missing. Wolves had already carried away five animals since lambing but none of them belonged to my master.

As I slept very little at night, I sometimes dozed off during the day taking only short naps since I was still responsible for my herd. On the day I had certainly overslept, I did not find my lambs when I woke up. I ran to the left and to the right: but there was nothing. Tired of looking in vain, I went back to the camp to warn my master – and all the way home, I was shaking from fear. If they were lost, I would be killed! And there, at the campsite, I found my master with all the lambs, who had returned home on their own.

My master, nevertheless, took a heavy stick and beat me so hard I suffered terrible pains for many days. I was definitely worthless, a filthy *giavour*, and a slave. I knew I deserved my punishment, but to me it seemed disproportionate, considering the meager advantages I received for my work.

From that time, when I felt I could not stay awake at night, I stopped giving the ritual signal to acknowledge my presence. The shepherds would then call me, but I would not answer. They would think I was asleep, and thus were forced to take over my watch. I felt relieved, and peacefully slept through the night. In the morning when we all met, the shepherds scolded me, but they all used my strategy in turn to find some rest!

XXVI

Another night, while we were peacefully keeping our lambs, we heard a call, *"Haaho! Haaho!"* (meaning "Help! Help!"). The voices came from far behind us, where the shepherds were staying. We, the lamb shepherds, kept our herds rather close to the campsite, but we still heard the alarm. In turn, we screamed, *"Haaho! Haaho!"* to warn the tent village. A few moments later, the sound of horsemen going full gallop echoed in the wide plain. They were firing and yelling, *"Vail lo! Vail lo!"* The night surrounded us and we could not tell where they were heading. Soon after, the commotion subsided and all became silent again.

The following day, I asked my master what had happened. He told me looters had tried to steal the sheep, but the roar and the shooting of the horsemen had quickly scattered them. He also acknowledged that the silence of the night had amplified their action to their advantage. He told me that sometimes robbers would arrive in a large aggressive number: each camel would be mounted by two men, seated back to back, allowing them to shoot in all directions. They were highly dangerous and very difficult to fight. These attacks explained why the different herd-owners were gathered in common tent villages.

During the lamb nursing, I rarely saw Cheko; it was only for less than an hour a day, and our masters were always nearby while he was busy milking the ewes. The spring had arrived, and the time had come to go back to Aghmughara. My master's brother had hired an Arab shepherd for his lambs, and we soon became friends (even though we both spoke different languages). In the long run, we understood each other. We often walked side by side and he told me about this country, which he knew well. When we left Mesopotamia, we finally came across Kurdish villages – where we begged for some bread, saying that we had been separated from our caravan, and thus were without any food supply. We lamb shepherds, alas, could not even satiate our hunger by sucking the milk of ewes!

The closer we got to Aghmughara, the faster we walked. We arrived at the village after four to five months of absence. I had been excited to leave and I was even more excited to be back. Without delay, I paid a visit to all the Kurds I knew. One of them, married to an Armenian woman, was kind to me. Usually, when someone died in the village, he was the one called upon to dig the grave. But he had died during the winter and people started whispering gossip to my master's ears. "When this man dug your brother's grave, we heard him say how good it was for a rich man to die once in a while, because it was time for a feast." In fact, it was the custom to end the funeral service with a meal, according to people's means. Of course, when my master's brother died, the feast was particularly opulent. My master burst into a rage and declared, "Why didn't you tell me this before his death? I would have crushed his head!" He was slapping his hand flat on his knee with violence, adding, "Ha! If only you could still be alive, I would show you who I am!" And my master became sick for a month after this news.

I took advantage of this lapse of time to visit my two Armenian friends. Not only was I eager to see them, but I had to share the great news Cheko had told me – about the orphanage in Urfa. They had also been informed.

Since then, I tried my best to convince them to join me in the escape. Hamed Ali did not want to hear a word about it. The other one, however, agreed – but he wanted more time, until after the harvest. "If you wait till we've done our hardest work, then you'd better give up," I used to tell him. The village was full of gossips and everyone was asking me, "So, Azo, aren't you going with the *giavours*?" "I am a Muslim, I won't go!" was my answer. Of course, I was hiding the truth, and I had to behave with great caution, knowing how difficult it would be to free myself from my terrible master.

XXVII

At this time, I kept the lambs at night with my master's brother's two shepherds. One was Arab (the one I mentioned before), and the other a Kurdish refugee whom I had met on my very first night at my master's. The three of us were young and careless and used to sleep during our watch. Very often, we woke up and our lambs would be gone. The large group had moved during our sleep. What should we have done then? Should we have run away in fear of retaliation? Or should we have gone down to alert the village? Fortunately, we often found them in the morning after quite a long search; or, more often, other shepherds showed us the place where our lambs were grazing. They had gained weight with the fresh grass they had enjoyed during those nights. However, I was getting worried because our carelessness had its share of risks. What if wolves had met them and slaughtered them? What if gangs of thieves had crossed their road and stolen them? Our masters would have rightly, but severely punished us. What about me, the *giavour*? I felt much more exposed than the two others. In fact, I felt threatened.

My master decided to go to Urfa. For me, this city meant hope, a light of freedom. All the good news was coming from Urfa: the war was ending; the English had arrived, bringing safety to the region; and the Armenians, who had escaped the slaughters, were gathered in all the surrounding cities. I was watching my master get ready for his journey with a burning demand on my lips: "Take me with you!" But this could not be. I simply showed him my bare feet, as my boots were worn out. He promised to bring me a new pair and left.

One morning during his absence, while I was keeping my lambs at the edge of a wheat field, I fell asleep. I suddenly woke up and realized that most of my lambs were grazing in it. At the same time, the field owner was darting towards me in a great rage. I quickly jumped to my feet and moved the lambs out of the field. The man, a sturdy fellow, yelled and threatened to beat me up if this happened again. Two hours later, I fell asleep again. Once again, I suddenly woke up and realized that all my lambs were grazing in most of his field. But this time, the owner was above me, holding a big stick ready to hit me. I managed to avoid the blow and took to my heels, leaving my lambs and all the rest. I ran and ran, driven by fear. After a long period of time, I slowed down. I realized then that I had run away from my village, and that the fear of being beaten had served my plan. I decided to keep going until I reached the next village, which I could see on the other side of the hill. I walked a long time. The daylight was fading away. The night came quickly and as I heard steps and voices approaching me, I jumped and hid in a ditch nearby. The voices passed over my head. Several women were talking and complaining about the poor milking of the day. When they had left, I came out of my hiding place and resumed my walk. Finally, I reached the village, which was unknown to me. I could barely see because of the dark and moved forward with caution. At the first house I saw, I asked permission to spend the night. The man stared at me and asked who I was and where I was coming from. I told him I was coming from far away and had left my master after a quarrel. "What's his name?" asked the man. "Khalil and he lives in Bozdepe," I answered boldly. He repeated the name several times, "Khalil, Khalil, I seem to know this name. He is known to be a severe man. You can stay here tonight and if you want, tomorrow morning, you will go with this young man (his guest) to the next village. I have a friend who needs a goat keeper."

I remembered that four years earlier, between this village and Aghmughara, the Kurd had carried away my sister, and had left my sick mother practically naked. I started to explain that I had come to this region to find my sister, as we had been separated four years ago. I wanted to know if he had heard about her. He thought about it and said he did not know her. He had, however, heard that in a village in the region of Kurdey was a foreign girl, but he did not know whether she was still there or not. Later, he asked his wife to give me some soup, and then pointed to a corner of the room where I could spend the night.

XXVIII

As agreed, I left with the young man early in the morning. I was doing so to show gratitude for the hospitality I had received. However, the direction we took was not the road to Urfa, which was what I had in mind. I told him I was looking for my sister and that she could not be in the direction we were heading. It was better to separate our paths, which we did. After walking many hours, I reached an intersection of two roads, one of which led to

Urfa. I became hesitant and even suspicious: What if my master suddenly appeared on his horse! I would be taken back and forced to abandon my plan! I looked toward the other side and saw two young people, a man and a woman, plowing in a field. I approached them and told them I was looking for my sister, so I could go to Urfa with her. They answered that they did not know anyone that could fit my description of her. As they were sowing corn, I kept staring at their work – and turning to the young woman, I told her, "You are not doing it correctly!" Taking a handful of grains, I showed her the right way. They both admired my skill and confessed they did not have much experience. They were brother and sister. Their father had just died and their mother was at home. The man asked me if I would agree to stay with them. I was facing the dilemma of working in a field or continuing my road to Urfa alone. I thought about it. They seemed young, friendly, and trustful. I decided to stay and told them so. Immediately, the young woman returned to the village, pleased that such a good deal relieved her from field labor. It was obvious she took no liking to it. And here I was, sowing grains of corn with a new master, who looked delighted and grateful.

We worked all day and when the evening arrived, my young master led me to his home. He introduced me to his mother, who welcomed me with a bright smile, congratulating me for my skill. We were all together, having a nice dinner made of soup and bread, when a neighbor came in. She told us that this very day, an armed horseman had come to the village looking for someone like me. She said nobody knew about me, so no information was given away. I was shivering with fear and thought my time had come, but I remained silent.

The following day, we left early to go to the field. I trusted my young master, so I confided all my worries to him, hoping for some help. He told me he would send me to some friends of his in a village where no one could find me. I asked him how I could reach Urfa and he replied, "It is very complicated to go to Urfa. You will get lost and the road is difficult."

The next day, there we were again, tilling the field. My master had planned to finish the work by noon, rest in the afternoon, and leave the next morning at daybreak. I had decided to leave right after lunch and not postpone my departure any longer. I knew how obstinate and terrible my old masters were.

As soon as we had relieved the oxen on our way back home, I turned around, not knowing why, and saw that behind us was a man, riding a white horse on the side of the hill. He was coming in our direction and I immediately panicked, "This man is looking for me!" My master advised me to hide in the wheat field alongside the road. I squatted in the depth of the stalks, which were already quite tall. A few minutes later, I heard the terrible voice of my old master's brother, "Lo, Azo, Azo!" He repeated my name several times, with a distinct mark of impatience. I had been betrayed and I was forced to surrender. I stood up at once, my head sticking out of the field of moving stalks. The horse got scared and reared itself up. The man, undisturbed, ordered me to come, grabbed me by the arm, and lifted me on his horse behind him.

Here I was, back to the horrible state of slavery I was desperate to escape. My young former master had watched the whole scene, dumbfounded. He must have yielded under the threat of the weapon carried by the horseman. I wanted to tell him, "I do not bear any grudge against you. I will find another opportunity to run away!" The horse was whipped and off we were at full gallop. The young man kept following us with his eyes, as far as he could. No doubt he felt sorry and sad, but thanks to me, his whole field had been sowed. As for me, everything had to be done – and I dreaded the punishment that was to come.

XXIX

We finally reached Aghmughara. My master was not back from Urfa yet. My mistress was quite beside herself: an absent husband and a slave on the run. I explained my unfortunate encounter with the owner of the wheat field, to everyone in the household. I described the terror I felt when, awakening from my sleep, I saw a man above my face with a large stick. I had run away, but with no intention of fleeing. Everybody thought I had been severely beaten, in spite of the man's vigorous denials. In fact, my adventure got largely spread around the village and fed all the gossip.

A couple of days later, my master came back from Urfa and was quickly informed of my escape. He immediately picked up his gun, grabbed me by the arm, and forced me outside of the house. "You wanted to flee while I was gone!" He struck me with a violent blow to the face. Afterward, he pointed to the gun and added, "If you try one more time to run away . . . You hear me? I will kill you with one bullet – only one – because you are not worth two bullets!" He went back inside, hung his gun, and returned with a pair of short boots. He threw them at me and said, "Here – for you, but you do not deserve them!"

I put on my new boots and left in tears – and in a state of shock. I went to meet my lambs, that luckily had been gathered by another shepherd. I kept watching them live in their innocence, being informed of nothing. They came to rub against me and lick my legs. I understood they had missed me. They liked me and knew my voice well, because I used to talk to them, telling them all the distress of my life.

I went to see Cheko, who advised me to wait until the lambs would be mixed with the sheep. Days went by and as they grew stronger, my lambs were soon weaned. They had lost the smell of their mothers and could not recognize them. I was being patient and striving to have my escape attempt forgotten. But more than ever, I was intent on leaving this horrible place.

XXX

The farmers had begun the harvest. One afternoon, as I was with my lambs at the edge of a wheat field, I felt the sudden urge to eat roasted wheat, the way Kurds prepared it. I collected some dried-out grass in a heap and pulled out a bunch of ripe ears of wheat. I started a fire, placing the ears over it to toast them. But a brisk wind started blowing, scattering the fire around and spreading it quickly to the dry grass. I tried to stop it but I had nothing to use except my shirt, held at the waist by a string full of knots. What could I do? The fire was heading straight to the wheat field with renewed strength. I could not run away; I would be caught immediately. I then decided to call for help at the top of my lungs, "Haho! Haho! Haho! Haho!" A man arrived at full speed, removed his top garment, and struck the fire with it without looking at me. He was the owner of the field! He kept on striking and yelling in a loud voice, *"Ya guidichey, Abdelkhader! Ya guidichey Abdelkhader!"* (Abdelkhader, O prophet, protect my crop!)

My calls had reached far away. Farmers who were working in their fields and inhabitants from surrounding villages were all running to help. Some were carrying sticks, others had cutlasses, or even hatchets. Luckily, the fire was almost extinguished, thanks to the owner's efforts and swift reaction. Some villagers were laughing, relieved to discover that the danger had been avoided; others were eating my roasted grain, finding the taste to their liking; some were saying I deserved to be punished, while others were praising my self-control and my call for help. Everyone was voicing their opinions and the continuing discussion helped to create or renew bonds among them. I was left alone, squatted down in a corner, looking sheepish, and acting grieved – mainly regretting the good meal I had missed. I did not dare say a word, because my situation was still up in the air and could turn one way or the other. I was not moving an inch until they all dispersed. Then, I went back to my lambs, my eyes swollen with tears and my heart pounding with anxiety. It had been a very depressing day.

Days and weeks went by, interrupted only by small events, until the morning when our master sent the order to mix the lambs with the sheep. The following night, I was working with Cheko, leading the sheep to pasture, feeling pleased and lighthearted. I told my friend all the resentment I bore and the hope I nurtured, thanking him for his good advice. I shared my plan to run away that very night, but he did not approve of my decision. Besides, I was already frightened by the idea of walking alone in the dark. Cheko told me it would be better to leave during the daytime: it would give us time to get organized and erase all traces of complicity between us in my escape.

He added, "Tomorrow, you must ask Khatoon to let you take the sheep all alone to the pasture. You'll lead them to the high hill in front of us and you'll stop the flock on the slope facing the village. From the village, I'll keep an eye open, ready to step in, in case I notice the sheep are becoming scattered. I will then tell the master you must have fallen asleep as usual, and that I have to go and check up on it. Of course, you'll have been gone a long time before and I would just replace you, warning the master only at sunset. I'll pretend that you fell asleep, but were much too afraid to come back to the village because of retaliation. During that day, you'll have plenty of time to gain a comfortable lead, and I'll divert the master's attention as long as I can."

We agreed on this plan. We gathered our sheep to put them to sleep instead of grazing, to gain some night rest. Our master would not find out, no more than usual. At daybreak, completely restored, we led our flock to a new pasture where the grass was amazingly thick. The sheep found abundant food without moving much, and Cheko predicted that our mistress would get a nice milking. The sun was already high in the sky and the heat was intense.

It was time to get back to the village, as we did every morning. Cheko was right: our mistress was pleasantly surprised to collect so much milk. As she was very content, I took advantage of the situation to declare, "It's a little bit thanks to me that you have collected so much milk. I know a place where the grass is rich and thick. If Khatoon would allow me, I'll go alone with my sheep in a short while and you'll see next morning how much milk you'll have." As I expected, she agreed and said, "Haydey, Azo, I want you to put Cheko to shame!" "Of course, dear Khatoon," I replied. "But where I intend to go, there are lots of thorns. My shoes are completely worn out and I won't be able to walk to reach the place. Can I borrow your shoes just for the day?" She immediately removed her shoes and gave them to me. Cheko, who was watching the scene, was biting his tongue not to say a word. I could see in his eyes how glad he was for me to go, but he could hardly hide the sadness of losing his best friend. My mistress then walked away. We were left alone for a few minutes. He looked at me, his eyes overflowing with friendship; his body stiffened by emotion; and he barely touched the hand I was stretching. I knew what kind of act he had to put on to delay our master's decision to go after me – and I knew it could be to his detriment. Following this quick farewell, I gathered my sheep and as agreed, left toward the pasture. Cheko remained seated by the tent facing the high hill, and as promised, would stay there to watch over my flock.

When I arrived on the slope facing the village, I left my herd and kept walking. After a short distance, I started trembling, overwhelmed by fear. "If they catch me, they'll kill me this time and I know I am not worth more than a bullet!" I was so disturbed that I turned around and walked back, telling myself I could wait another day or for a better opportunity, involving less risk. But an inner strength came over me saying, "Go! You must go! You have suffered enough! Go!" I was bewildered and did not know which decision to make. I stood there as if paralysed – halfway between the place that meant temporary security and the warmth of my sheep – and the road to freedom. I was captivated by the voice that became louder and ordered me to go. All of a sudden, I felt strong and full of renewed courage. I checked around me to see if someone was there. I could only see my sheep far away, grazing peacefully. Nobody knew what I was about to attempt, except my brave friend, who was faithfully standing next to the tent and who had trusted me. Then, I raised my arms over the animals I knew so well and loved so much, with whom I lived and slept so many days and nights – and said, "Farewell, my dear sheep and lambs, my friends, farewell! Farewell, hills and mountains, farewell to you, too, because I'm going and I'll never see you again!" Painfully, I broke away from the little bit of sweetness and softness I had found during my slavery. I pulled myself away from this long and tearful goodbye and left forever. When I finally looked back, I could no longer see my flock.

XXXI

I started walking faster and covered many miles quite rapidly. I knew that my master would organize the search by sending several men to the surrounding villages to collect information. They would come back to report and share their results. Then, they would leave together in the direction that seemed to be the most likely one to find me, based on their investigations. So I had to maintain the longest distance possible between myself and my pursuers.

As I was afraid to turn right, which was the road to Urfa, I turned left. However, according to my judgment, this road would not take me too far away from my destination. The first village I saw was named Kergoo. To be safe, I did not go through it, but went around it, across the fields. A man who was working did not even notice me. I kept on walking with less fear, thinking the biggest danger of being caught had been avoided. I continued without stopping and finally reached another village by the name of Djimbolat. I entered it, and a woman holding a basket passed next to me,grumbling, "Look at this runaway *giavour* wearing his mistress's shoes!" I let the accusation go by without reacting, even though I was deeply surprised by the sharpness of her comment. I continued walking with almost no fear now, convinced I had taken all the necessary precautions. I went straight to the well and saw a large mulberry tree next to it. The sight of this tree, on my road to freedom, filled my heart with great joy. Many sweet memories came back to me: memories of my country, of my home, and of my garden, where this type of tree grew in abundance. It was the first time since my captivity that I had seen a mulberry tree. It was covered with fruit that was not completely ripe. So what! I climbed up and devoured as many berries as I could to fill my starving stomach.

The sun was setting and it was nearly night time. I had to stop somewhere soon. I went back to the road and continued my journey. After a short while, I came to an intersection. On my left, I could see a village, much too far to reach before dark. I decided to go right, guessing that the road would take me to a village that was not yet in sight. In this type of region, there were no isolated houses between villages. For reasons of security, the inhabitants gathered in clusters, sometimes very far from one another. Only fields and hills were visible from one hamlet to the next. I walked some more and had to climb up a hill, where I desperately hoped to find shelter quickly. Finally, I saw the first house. The night was getting so dark and I was so exhausted, that I went directly to the door to beg for a place to sleep. The lady looked at me carefully, asked me a few questions, then let me in. I felt I was in good hands so I told her the truth: I was a *giavour*, I had run away from my master because of my harsh living conditions. She pitied me and told me, "Before we used to live in Suruj. If only I had met you, I would have kept you." She then showed me the road to take in the morning, advising me not to stop at the first village but the next one – by the name of Havag. The people were quite friendly there, and I would certainly find a place to work. Then, some curious neighbors came over. Some offered me jobs, but I refused politely. "I need to get as far away as possible. If I get caught, it's certain death for me." "Lo! I hear a horseman coming!" someone said to scare me. They all laughed heartily, not meaning any harm. I asked them the name of their village. "Kurdey" they answered. I told them about my sister, and how I had been trying to find her for many years. I had heard she could be in this village. They said they did not know of any young Armenian girl, and they had no *giavours* in their village. The woman served me some soup and showed me the place where I could spend the night.

I got up very early in the morning, ready to leave, but it started raining. The woman asked me to stay inside until the end of the rain and offered me some milk and butter. An hour later, I thanked her and left toward the road she had mentioned the night before. The weather was stormy and muggy but soon cleared up. After a few hours, the sun shone again and rapidly dried my shirt.

I arrived at the first village, Gharghash. As I had been told, I went around it and reached a crossroads on the other side of it. I did not know which direction to take. I saw a man working on the lower part of a roof, so I asked him the way to Havag. He pointed to it and immediately added, "Why don't you go to Urfa instead? All the *giavours* are gathered there and they are well treated." "I don't want to be with *giavours*!" was my answer, and I left. His comment did not go unnoticed. It filled my heart with courage and fortified my secret goal to reach Urfa. I went from one hill to another, and I knew I was very far from my master. I had walked a long way, taking less common roads to guard against the danger of being caught. I wondered when I would see Havag. Behind which of these hills hid the village which was so highly praised?

XXXII

I finally arrived at the foot of a high hill I had to climb. When I reached the top, an immense green valley opened up in front of my eyes. I had never seen such a beautiful sight since the beginning of my exile. I thought all the treasures of Paradise were unfolding at my feet. I took a deep breath and looked at this new land with feverish excitement, as if my soul had been in need of opulence and beauty. I slowly walked down the hill along a winding slope and found a spring that was feeding a large pond. I eagerly drank the fresh, cool water. Continuing on the path through the trees, I saw people carrying baskets loaded with red, white, and black berries. My heart went straight to my garden in Amasia where such fruit grew in profusion. "What a pity I had never suspected such a welcoming place existed! I would have immediately fled the arid and sterile region where I had been living in misery for so many years," I told myself. I walked along a garden where a full grown mulberry tree caught my eye. Although I was starving, I hesitated, since people were working close by. But how could I resist such a temptation? I made up my mind and in the blink of an eye, climbed up the tree, helping myself to berries. I had hardly tasted the delicious fruit when a man holding a long stick struck my feet and yelled, "Get down!

If you want to eat berries, go to the mulberry wood over there and eat as much as you want!"

Reluctantly, I climbed down, not knowing where the wood was located. I resumed my course, but no village was in sight. Where was Havag? Finally, after walking some more, I reached the entrance to the famous village. I crossed the streets at a slow pace, looking at the shop windows in total amazement. I had not seen such wonderful displays since Amasia. I arrived at a large square on the other side of the village. It was the area where large, freshly cut bundles of wheat had been heaped, ready for the threshing of grains. As I was exhausted and famished from my two full days of walking (all I had eaten was the soup which the Kurdish woman had given to me), I looked for the thickest bundle, thinking it would belong to the wealthiest farmer. A calf was eating out of the bundle, and I thought I would soon find out who the owner was! I sat in the shade, hiding from the intense heat, and waited for some action. The calf was out in the sun and visible to everyone. In seconds, I heard screams, and stones were falling around me. The calf fled and the farmer came running, checking to see if another calf was eating up his crop. He did not find any – but he found me! He stood before me and asked what I was doing there. I said I was just resting a little.

"You are a *giavour!*"

"*Elhamdoullah!*" (I'm a Muslim now)

"Where do you work?"

"Nowhere."

"Do you want to work for me?"

"How much do you pay?"

"What can you do to deserve a wage? Can you plow?"

"Of course I can!"

"Can you carry bales of straw?"

"No . . . but I can do anything else."

He was very shrewd and had proposed the two hardest tasks. He knew I could not carry such heavy weight! He then added, "If you stay with me, you'll be well-fed and well-dressed, and I'll buy you shoes." I accepted the offer and he took me to his place, a very comfortable one, not far from the square. He gave me plenty of food, and we were soon on good terms. He treated me like one of his sons, and I wondered why I had not met such generous masters before. I would have been comforted from the terrible loss of my family and would not have suffered as much. However, in spite of the good living conditions I was now enjoying, I never gave up the idea of leaving; I was determined to reach my goal.

XXXIII

My new master's name was Nebo. He had two sons who were attending school in the village. I was curious and kept looking at their books. I knew the letters but I could not read them. This surprised me because I could read Armenian and Turkish quite fluently. I soon realized the pages were excerpts from the Koran. The two sons were facing the same problem and had to learn most of their readings by heart. I had tears in my eyes, flashing back to my school books and notebooks. I remembered how my father had hoped that, one day, I would become a great man. His hope was not unfounded because I was more gifted than my brothers and sisters. For a split second, I imagined myself back home with my parents. I was in Paradise!

Nebo, who was my ninth master, owned vineyards, vegetable gardens, and orchards, thanks to the spring I had seen on the day of my arrival. Farmers were thus able to water their lands generously. Where I had come from, the scarce water could only be found in wells, and people lived in poverty. My master gave me a pair of oxen to look after, telling me specifically where I was allowed to go. I was free to eat as many berries as I wanted, and I did not restrict myself; in fact, I was catching up, after all those years of starvation!

Deep inside, I was still afraid my previous masters would find me. I did not want to be taken away from this new comfortable life. What was I supposed to do? I knew how rough and forceful they were and how they would search for their slave with determination. I thought this over and made up my mind to get to Urfa as soon as possible. To achieve my goal, I first had to look for boys who were living in the same situation as I was. I started my search.

I knew from hearsay that many young men were employed in the village. I found out that one of them, whom I had met several times, was like me. I would have never guessed. He always wore a cutlass at his belt, was well-dressed, and walked with pride. He was a shepherd, like me. When I questioned him about his past, his face reddened, he became ill at ease, and finally admitted he was a *giavour*. I told him about my plan to go to Urfa, but I did not know how to get there. He did know, so I then suggested we could go together. He refused and acted embarrassed. Each time I would see him, I would ask again and repeat my offer – begging. And each time he would refuse. He told me, "Why don't you go with our fellow countryman who lives next door to your master? So far as I'm concerned, I'm staying!" I could see he was frightened, or that he did not trust me enough. My neighbor, who I used to see every day, was my age and my size. His name was Resho. He appeared to be in good shape and good health. First, I started to gain his confidence and get on friendly terms with him. He told me he had been working for five years in the same village and for the same master, who treated him like his own son. He did not want to leave him. He added that many Armenian children and teenagers had been gathered and sent to the orphanage, while others had run away from their masters. He knew the road to Urfa quite well and had walked over there twice, on a one-day trip. I was pleased to realize that having come all the way from Aghmughara, I had now brought myself closer to my destination. Urfa could be reached without an overnight stop. Each time I met Resho, I tried to convince him to come with me. One day, he finally agreed – and I was delighted!

A rumor spread that two Armenian youths had run away, taking their masters' money with them. This incident forced us to postpone our departure. Two weeks later, two more fled. The handsome young man with the cutlass at his belt was no longer in sight. I came to the conclusion that he was one of the last fugitives, and his strange behavior now made sense to me. I did not see my neighbor anymore. We avoided each other so no one could suspect we were plotting our escape. It was around that time that I became seriously ill, and our plan had to be delayed again. My master had to find someone else to thresh the wheat. It was an exhausting, three-week chore under an intense sun. I could not fathom how I would resume my job, considering my poor health. This hard work, in addition to the previous painful labor I had carried out for my other masters, was finally catching up with me. I was totally worn out. The local workers from the neighborhood, with whom I used to joke in Turkish, said, "Your master hired two *giavours* before you, and they are dead. Soon it will be your turn!"

As soon as I walked, the left side of my stomach swelled, and I had to stop. I was told my spleen was swelling. An old lady was giving me some massages and I was confined to bed for at least ten days, which really was to my master's displeasure. When, finally, I was barely able to stand on my feet, my master sent me to work immediately. One day, as I was in the garden, a Kurd approached me and told me, "Lo, Azo, someone is looking for you." I got scared and asked him if it was a man on a horse. "No, he is on foot and comes from a nearby village." I thought it over very quickly. If this Kurd was sent by my masters, he wouldn't have come on foot. If I was in danger, I could always run to the police station we had in Havag for protection. I was still thinking, when the Kurd appeared in front of me and immediately challenged me. "*Lo, erzeghrkh zema bezenan beleykhi cholley diu berevi?*" (Why did you abandon the goats in the desert and run away?) I stared at him and answered, "*Lo diu divanei, bodalai ez de neconem!*" (You are totally insane, I don't know you at all!). But the man was insisting it was me. I said, "What? You can't even recognize the boy who, for many years, has been keeping your goats!" He answered, "Yes, I do! It's you!" I exclaimed, "*Lo Khodeo Khodeo es che belan et!*" (My God, my God, what an ordeal!) I then started giving him the detailed account of all the places I had worked and the names of all my masters, so he would leave me alone.

The first Kurd who had sent for me had stayed with us to arbitrate the discussion. He intervened and said, "Azo is telling you the truth. He has always given us the same detail about himself. I have no doubt he is right." The other Kurd, who had certainly become insane after the loss of his goats, hesitated and left angrily. I thought that this crazy man could very well keep on inquiring all the way to Aghmughara. The news of my being at Havag could reach my previous master's ears and I would be discovered!

XXXIV

My master hired a worker to help thresh the wheat grains. He slept next to me on the ground in the open air. At the end of the second night of his arrival, I realized he had left. Once again, all the chores fell on me. The manual labor was not steady: the war had ended and everyone had to manage accordingly. My master, who was unable to replace him and could only rely on me to do the work, decided to speed up my recovery. He asked me to sleep inside his house, and I was very displeased. All my chances of escaping would be jeopardized. In the house, the hall opened up to a large reception room to welcome the guests and was covered with thick wool carpets. That was where I was going to sleep. As for my master and his wife, they were sharing another room, furnished with a large wooden bed.

During heat waves, people slept on their flat roofs. The peacefulness of the nights under the stars was sometimes disturbed by quarrels and retaliations. That was how a conflict arose when a young man from our village eloped with a young girl from another one. Gunshots were fired from all parts and mainly from the flat roofs. In these regions, the custom was to allow the girl to be engaged only with an exchange of presents. Their value was estimated according to many factors, and the age of the future spouses was significant. Thus, young but poor lovers, unable to afford this payment for their wedding, would often kidnap the young girls – usually with their consent. This explained the murderous revenges of the frustrated and disgraced families. The conflict could last several days to a week, and during that period of hostility all the roofs were deserted. Everyone had cautiously withdrawn inside their houses.

My master was in a constant rage. He could not find a worker to thresh his grains and he was obsessed by it. I knew the whole task would fall on me, and I was not up to it physically. For this reason, my friend and I agreed to run away, just before the beginning of the heavy work. One morning, my master ordered me to prepare the oxen and the plows so that the work could start early the following day. I asked for permission to sleep outside, next to the threshing grounds, so I could be on the premises at dawn for the job. He agreed. Late that evening, I lay on the straw and the night was quickly turning dark. As I waited for my friend Resho to come, I became extremely anxious about even the slightest noise I could hear. He finally arrived, as swiftly as a cat. I immediately saw how troubled he was. I guessed he was lacking the courage to carry out our plan. I convinced him again and told him he needed a few hours of sleep to build up some strength. Finally, I was the one to fall asleep, and I did not know for how long, until he woke me up. Resho had not slept a wink, as he was not used to sleeping on the ground. He proposed that we go to his place. In his master's garden, he had built a kind of elevated wooden platform on beams, surrounded by greenery on all sides. Very quietly, we climbed up to his sleeping quarters, which consisted of a mattress covered with a wool blanket. There, Resho was comfortable and fell asleep immediately – but I could not. The mattress had a strange smell which made me nauseous. I was no longer used to the softness of a blanket, and I had lost the habit of sleeping on a bed since my captivity. So as soon as my friend put his head on the pillow, he fell into a deep sleep, and I was the one to lie awake. My heart was pounding. Were we about to throw away this opportunity to escape? Our lives were at risk! Lying on my back with my eyes wide open, I evaluated all the options we had to achieve our scheme. This night was the one. We had to reach Urfa together, and we had to leave tonight.

I finally dozed on and off, overcome by fatigue. I lost all track of time and could not tell how late it actually was, on this very night which held all of our hopes! I shook my friend, who was sleeping like a log, and whispered in his ear, "Wake up and let's go! Time's up!" He barely opened his eyes and noticing only darkness around him, he said, "It's too dark! We can't see a thing! It couldn't be more than midnight, so let me sleep some more!" He went back to his dreams. I was petrified I would do the same, as I was exhausted from stress and worry – and my head was feeling so heavy.

XXXV

I woke up with a start and was immediately wide awake. The crow of a rooster close by stirred the silence of the night. I leaned over my friend, "Lo, Resho, Resho . . . get up, get up!" He sat up with difficulty, while the rooster's *cock-a-doodle-doo* echoed again in the distance. I jostled Resho a little and at last, we climbed down from the perched bed. This escape seemed more to me like a dream than a reality.

He knew all the safe roads bordering gardens and vineyards. He took the lead and I followed behind him. In the darkness, trees appeared to me like armed soldiers on sentry duty. I was walking with difficulty because of the excruciating pain, but I remained silent so I would not discourage my friend. We finally reached the main road without any problems. There, I begged him to stop for a while. Although I had held my stomach tightly with my two hands, the pain was taking my breath away, and I felt truly exhausted. Resho then started to cry and whine, "What a stupid thing we did to leave together! With you, we'll never make it!"

We had left the village an hour earlier, and the sun was already rising. After a short period of rest, I felt stronger, and we resumed our walk very slowly. Resho was still consumed by anxiety and regrets: "I should have never left! They're going to catch us!" I comforted him as best as I could. "Don't worry! They must believe we left a long time ago, and that we're already in Urfa." Without realizing it, I was walking a touch faster. We kept looking behind us to make sure we were not being followed.

After a three to four hour walk, Resho told me, "When we reach Mount Dolametch, I'll no longer be scared." The mountain was standing right in front of us, and the climb appeared to be a difficult one. But God seemed to have given me some supernatural strength, for I reached the top without too much pain. Resho started to smile, feeling relieved and confident.

After crossing the mountain, we met two Kurds with their donkeys, which were loaded with provisions. The little convoy was also going to Urfa. We joined them and kept chatting on a friendly basis. Thus, while helping them escort their donkeys, we kind of mingled with the group to gain some protection. They quickly guessed who we were and asked us if we would stay with them. They were two brothers, who each offered to become responsible for us. We refused. We did not want to be tied to anyone; we just wanted to reach Urfa. After a short while, they sat under a tree to have lunch, so it must have been around noon. We also sat a little further away to rest, watching them eat, and feeling terribly thirsty and hungry. They felt sorry for us – we looked so deprived of everything – and thus gave us some bread and cheese. We decided to stay with them because they were bringing us the safety we needed.

We resumed our journey and after a long walk, we arrived at a place called Achkh Sou, which means "the open spring." There, travelers and caravan drivers would stop to get some fresh water and rest. The spring was surrounded by a large number of men and animals. Our road mates stopped, too, and we all drank to our fill. To our delight, Resho, who owned two *kurush*, bought some grapes.

The two Kurds moved on, and we followed them as intended. As for me, my legs were giving up and I had the hardest time standing. I was overwhelmed by the side effects of my disease and the extreme fatigue. However, thanks to my powerful mental state, strengthened by our proximity to Urfa, I managed to stand up and keep going. We soon could see the minarets of Urfa, which we hoped to reach within an hour. As we walked, we were overlooking a valley. We finally caught up with the two Kurds, who told us that during the deportations, this large valley was covered with bodies of *giavours*. I started trembling with fear, remembering the atrocious scenes I myself had witnessed. Here too, my people had been massacred. The intense joy that was supposed to illuminate my heart and my soul upon my arrival suddenly became grief – and my eyes could not detach

Urfa, where Papken found sanctuary.

themselves from this sinister valley, where so many lives had been exterminated.

We had almost reached the gates of Urfa, so we let the two Kurdish brothers continue their journey on their own. There was a door open at a mill, which stood next to a large building. As Resho could not speak a word of Turkish, I entered and found myself in a sort of laundry room, where soldiers were washing their clothes. I came closer and realized I could not understand their language. I knew that Urfa had been occupied by the British, but where did these men with dark skin and turbaned heads come from? What should I do? Who should I talk to? A little further down, some men were building a house in the middle of a large lot. I also noticed a young lady dressed in European style, standing in a field. I walked towards her, greeted her, and asked her in Turkish where the orphanage was. Although she did not seem to understand the language of my question, she had guessed its meaning and pointed to the right part of the city. There was still a good distance to go. I went back to the road where Resho was waiting for me. We soon came across a group of young Turks. They cursed us, insulted us, and we were afraid they were going to beat us. They left, but their aggressive attitude had drawn an old man's attention. He was passing by with his donkey, heavily loaded with two wicker baskets full of grapes. The old man, who was a little ahead of us, turned around and waited. He wanted to know if we were Armenians. We said we were. He then remarked, "I'll help you find the orphanage, but first have some grapes!" and he gave each of us a generous handful of them. We were overjoyed. Without saying another word, he walked in front of us in a hurry and guided us through the streets of Urfa. We followed him with great difficulty. After many turns, we finally arrived in front of a large entrance door where a guard was standing. Our benefactor left us to the guard's care and immediately proceeded on his way. Could he have been Armenian? This remained a mystery.

At last, I had reached the orphanage . . . the haven . . . the home I had desperately dreamed about. How many troubles and how much misery had I endured to arrive here! I thanked our Lord for his mercy and stepped through the doorway of the orphanage, beaming with joy. Walking through the gates of heaven would not have made me happier!

XXXVI

Resho and I entered the orphanage. The guard led us through several large buildings, a first courtyard, then a second one which was much smaller. We climbed up a narrow staircase and were asked to wait at the door. Finally, a heavyset, white-haired old lady with glasses, which was a sign of a rare distinction, came out. Her glasses were sparkling in the sunlight. She was with an interpreter who was holding a notepad in her hands. She started to question us in Armenian. I answered in Turkish telling her we had lost the use of our mother tongue but that we both spoke

Kurdish, and I could speak Turkish quite well. She then asked her questions in that language:

"Where do you come from?"

"We both ran away from the Kurds!"

"What are your names?"

"Papken Injarabian, I was born in Amasia. My friend is Herant Duriguerian and he is from Sivas."

She wrote down the information. All of a sudden, very worried and disoriented, Resho and I looked at each other and started to blush. I whispered in his ear in Kurdish, so no one could understand us, "We will keep our promise! We are not and we'll never become *giavours*! We'll always be Muslims!" I then wondered why I was so determined to remain a Muslim. A shiver ran through me. Only an obscure threat could explain this choice. I did not want to be known as a *giavour*, the most worthless human being on earth, the lowest of them all. Resho and I were overcome by shame and distress. The registration was in order so we went down the narrow stairs. In the yard, we sat on the ground and were given a small loaf of bread with cheese. We were starving and swallowed the meager meal in no time. Boys and girls started to crowd around us. They were all asking questions. They hoped we could bring them news from one of their relatives lost during the deportation. I myself expected to find someone I knew among them, but I did not recognize any familiar face. I thought they all must be dead! Resho was more fortunate and recognized some friends and classmates.

At the end of our meal, we were led to a large washroom where water was heating up in huge pots above a wooden fire. Some women, whose jobs were to bathe the orphans, were waiting for us. One of them grabbed me by the arm, turned me around, and looked at me attentively. "You come from Aghmughara?" A little surprised, I nodded. With tears in her eyes, she told me, "I am Mariam, your master Ibrahim Bekir's brother's servant!" Tears of joy were rolling down her face. Mariam was the very person who had witnessed my misery and knew the darkness of my story: my arrival at the village with my mother and sister, and the Kurd who would carry her away forever. Mariam was like my angel, who helped me before and was here to help me again. I said, "The Kurds told me you were dead!" "You can see, I am alive and well!" she answered with a large smile.

I undressed and my rags were thrown out in the garbage. They made me sit on a bench and two women began washing me. They were saying, "Good Lord, how filthy he is!" A little further away, Resho was suffering the same fate. They scrubbed the dirt off me using large quantities of water and soap. They rubbed me so well that I became as white as a newborn baby. I could not recall ever washing myself during my years with the Kurds. Then, very startled, I put on a perfectly clean shirt and underwear. Some boys were playing ball with the skullcap I was wearing when I first arrived. I wished I could have kept it as a souvenir of my captivity. It had been given to me by my last master. For two or three days, Mariam managed to keep me next to her, a special favor that had been granted to her. Then, I was led to the boys' dormitory. It was not a very large room. On the floor, wool mattresses were set against one another and I had to make one of them mine. It was very hot and the smell of this room turned my stomach. I had only one desire: to sleep wrapped in my blanket by the window where I could breathe some fresh air from outside. As I was sick and confined to the dorm, I saw nobody all day, except a few other orphans, sick like me.

I had made my way to the orphanage through great efforts and I was now completely exhausted. I stayed in bed and every day, Mariam would bring me yogurt and medicine. After a couple of weeks, I could stand up and walk around, but I did not meet any of the children. I asked Mariam, "Where are the orphans? The day of my arrival, the playground was full of them." She answered, "Because it was on a Sunday." I thought that Sunday had been a great day! I did not realize then that our Lord had given us his protection and had led us to this place exactly on a Sunday. I had left Amasia on June 21, 1915; I had reached the orphanage of Urfa on a Sunday, in the year 1919, around the end of July or the beginning of August.

I did not see Resho anymore. He had probably forgotten me. Mariam told me she had met him and he seemed to be doing well. The younger orphans were attending class; the older ones were working at the entrance of the village, preparing the ground in an area that belonged to the orphanage. It was the place where I had asked directions from the young European lady.

Mariam advised me to rest until I had completely recovered, which I did; I was getting stronger every day. I started to become familiar with the layout of the big orphanage, which was built on a soft slope. I soon noticed a slim, handsome, smiling young man who walked with a cane. Although I met him every day at the infirmary and was eager to have him as a friend, I dared not speak to him. One day, I gathered my courage to greet him and ask him about his legs. We soon became friends. I told him who I was, where I was from, and what misfortunes I had been through. He then told me his story and how he had escaped death:

"In the caravan where I was, no adult nor living men were left, only the young and the old ones. One day, the entire group was taken over by the Turks, and we all spent the night in jail. The following morning, with our hands tied behind our backs, they led us to the edge of a gorge and made us sit down in rows. Then, meticulously, they stripped us of our belongings, beheaded people one by one – without any trial – and tipped the mutilated bodies over the edge. My turn was coming up within four rows. Some curious Kurds had gathered around the seated victims and were calmly watching the executioners perform their sinister task. All of a sudden, one of them crawled to me, took a knife out and cut the rope that was tied to my hands and said, "You, *giavour*, you are going to die, let me have your jacket!" I was wearing a nice leather jacket, which he tore off my back and returned, crawling back. I could only realize one thing: my hands were untied and I was free. I started running and blindly threw myself into the gorge full of dying and dead bodies. The torturers shot at me and a bullet went through my two feet. I dug myself deeper among the bodies to hide. I could be seen no more and the firing stopped. This ravine was a mass grave where thousands of men had already met their death. I could hear all around me, cries of pain, moanings and whimpers. Then the night came and I fell asleep. I was awakened by screams and wailing. The sun was already high in the sky. The executioners and spectators were all gone. I crawled on my belly and got near the dying to free their hands. Some had their throats cut halfway through and were covered with blood. Finally, powerless, I decided to leave this hell and moved forward on my knees. For two to three days, although my suffering was extreme, I kept going and fed myself with growing herbs. I managed to reach a village and entered the first house in sight. A woman fed and took care of me. As soon as I was fit, I helped her the best I could until the day I decided, like you, to come here."

He told me his story with a smile on his face, while I listened, terrified and deeply moved. In fact, his story exceeded mine. I tried to fathom the level of blind violence that had been used to try and ruthlessly kill a handsome teenager of 15. It seemed incredible to me that mankind could commit such horrors. How could these executioners continue to live with peace of mind after such crimes? Was it possible that the notion of consciousness of one's own acts could not reach some men?

Finally, I recovered fully and joined the group of boys of a similar age. It was again on a Sunday when, for the first time, I met everybody in the main courtyard. Carefree and full of newfound happiness that belonged to their age, the orphans were playing together. Everyone else had playmates. I stood alone, having not yet overcome the suffering I had endured during my deportation. I looked sad and lonely.

XXXVII

Not far from me, I saw a well-dressed teenager pulling someone else's arm and urging him to come along. The other person refused and was struggling against him. He let go of him, and as I was right there, he asked me – with an encouraging smile – to follow him, calling me "brother" and softly holding my arm. I walked with him. I thought there were some chores to do, and I was willing to help since I felt stronger. However, it was not what I had thought. I climbed up some stairs behind him and entered a room that looked like a classroom with many benches. Children of different ages were seated. I was offered a spot. A bearded man was speaking to the audience in Turkish. But it was not the common Turkish language spoken in the streets. I could not understand the meaning of his words. I could only figure out that it was about grapes and wine. Then, the teenager who had brought me up, left and came back with somebody else. From where I was, I listened carefully, but still the words did not make sense. Later, I found out that we were gathered in this room to talk about God, to study the Bible, and to worship together.

Little by little, I felt that God's messages were coming alive inside me. I recognized our God of love and his powerful breath on that night when I was with my second master; I felt His presence all around me, which helped me rise and pray.

It was God who had led me to this room, it was He who had spared me from a death intended for all of my fellow countrymen. Later, I accepted His call and I converted. This was done with gentleness and consent, without any act of violence, whereas my so-called adherence to Islam had been subject to cruelty and threats of death. It was this overwhelming fear that had made me tell Resho, when we had reached the orphanage, "We'll always be Muslims."

At the same time that I was learning about God and his messages, I was attending regular classes. The school teacher handed me a book written in Armenian, and I became so emotional that tears filled my eyes. This one little book reminded me of my childhood, of my school, and family. My books were then thicker and I had many of them. I also used to own notebooks and colored pencils.

The use of my mother tongue came back quickly and I could soon read this book easily. In a very short time, I caught up with my friends. The teacher, however, required that only one or two pages should be read each day, when in fact, I could have read the whole book at once. I had no pen and no writing paper and reading was our sole exercise. I realized that the orphanage could not afford supplies for the newcomers. There was also a shortage of teachers.

I was eager only for one thing: to be educated. I wanted to read, write, and learn. But I had nothing. I picked up some lead I found on the ground and tied it between two pieces of wood. Here was my pencil! I collected slips of paper here and there. This poor supply helped me wait until the day real school equipment was given to me. However, our teacher did not have the adequate skills for our class level and for a long time, I made no progress.

The orphanage was like the Tower of Babel, where all the languages were spoken: Armenian, Turkish, Kurdish, Arabic,

Zaza and many others. I was looking for friends who could speak Kurdish. Very shortly, however, most of us became fluent in Armenian, since it was the language of our classes.

The morning sermon was delivered by Minister Djernazian, who was also the director of our boys' orphanage. He taught us prayers and hymns but was quickly replaced by a new director, Mr. Kevork Takavorian; he continued teaching us religious education, although he was not a minister.

Miss Mary Holmes, the woman with glasses who had welcomed Resho and me on the Sunday of our arrival, was the head director of the orphanage. She was American and previously was a missionary in Lebanon. Miss Holmes had been sent to Urfa by Near East Relief, an immense philanthropic foundation which worked wherever massacres had occurred. Tens of thousands of Armenian orphans had been placed under its protection.

XXXVIII

One day we were transferred to the new orphanage, where the older orphans had been working for some time. We were separated by age into groups of 25, with a designated leader, and settled under pyramid-like tents.

There, on that wide, open-space field, the orphans felt much closer to one another than before. The girls occupied the ground on one side and the boys on the other; in the middle stood a large administrative building, where Miss Holmes and all the secretaries worked.

Every morning, we would line up to return to the former center where general teaching and professional training were given. Our meals were also provided over there, and in the evening we would return to our campsite. We had a lot of space to move, to pray, to meet, and to get to know one another better.

Quite often, I would think about the orphans who remained in captivity, because they could not run away or because they were too fearful. I had great pity for them.

One Sunday at the campsite, I recognized the young fellow who had refused to escape with me a few months earlier. At that time, he was wearing a dagger on his belt. We spoke, and a little ashamed, he explained why he had declined to come along: a short time before I had revealed my plan and asked for his help, he had already promised another orphan to run away with him. They had both made it to Urfa safely, and he was sincerely happy to see me. He then asked me to come along and meet his friend.

Just then, another boy came to greet me. Where did I see him before? He told me, "I met you in Aghmughara. You were keeping your master's younger animals and you often walked past me. You would tie a rope to the horn of your tallest billy goat and move forward pulling on that rope, and the rest of the herd would follow." "Yes, I used to do that," I answered. He added, "I was keeping my master's sheep who had just arrived in the region. Do you remember? I am the one who advised you to go by Boshava, where life is better." He knew then, that I was Armenian, while I thought wrongly he was a Kurdish shepherd.

What had happened to Resho, my old pal? Very sociable, he had made many friends and was playing with everyone with renewed energy. I went over to talk to him. He was doing fine and was about to leave for Aleppo, where several members of his family were waiting for him. I told him how lucky he was to be reunited with them. Several orphans left under these conditions and I envied them – with no bitterness in my heart. I knew, alas, I had not a chance of hope!

It often happened when I was going downtown, that I would be stopped by women who believed I was their son. I had to give my name, explain my origins, and tell my story to convince them of their mistake. These were such sad encounters with mothers without children and children without mothers!

XXXIX

It was rumored that the British forces were about to depart and all Armenians would be affected by it. I saw the adults crying and they had good reason to be worried: the Turks feared the British. As soon as the British army would hear about fights or uprisings taking place in the city, the soldiers (most of them Indians) would readily climb up on the roofs and wave their colorful flags to reinstate order. It was a peaceful means of imposing their authority.

The Armenians were reassured by the British. "Do not lament, the French will soon come and take over," so it was said. But the Armenians did not have much confidence in their new protectors. The British left the city as of October 1919 and were replaced the same day by the French troops. Most of them were from North Africa and marched in the streets wearing fezes. Although the Turks were very pleased with the change, they greeted them with a cold welcome.

Our elders grew very worried but had to accept their fate, for better or for worse. As soon as the French got settled, public turmoils started in the shopping district, which was always in the midst of social unrest. The shop owners of all nationalities were often compelled to flee; they abandoned their stores and shelves, leaving them unprotected in order to find shelter at home. It was never clear who had stirred the riot and a general atmosphere of fear and insecurity prevailed.

Although the orphanage seemed to offer nice protection, we, the orphans, were very frightened. However, our youth helped us hope for a brighter future. In class, we studied "La Marseillaise," a very difficult exercise we learned as an act of faith. One morning, as the boys, the girls, and the teachers were all seated to eat, the head officer of the occupation troops – Commander Hugen – paid us a visit. He was a man of average height with a stocky build. The friendly and open look in his eyes made the strongest impression on us. He taught us the tune of "La Marseillaise" and we sang with the greatest enthusiasm after he had communicated his confidence in a swift victory.

During the morning of February 9, 1920, the conflict broke out between the Turks and the French. Since the night before, the orphans had left their campsite to return to their old lodgings, which offered a safer shelter. The Turks, who wanted to regain control of the city, opened fire and several rounds were exchanged across town; the noise of machine guns and cannons could be heard. It was very dangerous to go out. The food supply was almost depleted and we were all very hungry. We had had no time to anticipate and stock up on enough food – everything happened so fast. We were ordered to stay in our dormitories up to midday. Then, we were allowed to get up and each have a piece of bread with a bowl of hot water, where a few grains of cracked wheat were floating on the surface. Some of my friends fed upon raw grass. I wanted to do like them to dull the acute pain of hunger we all suffered, but I was still feeling too weak. How to leave the orphanage where all the exits were closed up, the windows condemned with rocks, and where guards were constantly patrolling the premises? After intense reflection, I found a way to go out. We opened a small hole in the wall and went through, one by one. We took turns and brought back all types of greenery. We ate the best of our miserable harvest, and those who could not take part because of health reasons had what was left.

Our going out, however, must have raised some attention, and we were soon ambushed. The Turks were shooting from the roofs, the minarets, from everywhere – and bullets were whistling all around us. I remember one of my friends catching one and burning his hand badly. Fortunately, we all managed to crawl back safely to our hole and reenter the orphanage.

XL

One morning, I decided to go out alone to explore further. I noticed daisies on a half-destroyed slanted roof. They had grown there wildly and were shining in the sunlight. I climbed on tumbled stones and started collecting them. I filled up my mouth and, while I was chewing, stuffed more into my pockets in a hurry. An Armenian guard armed with a rifle saw the danger I was exposed to and yelled at me, "Come down quickly! Come down this way! You'll get killed!" I was indeed a perfect target for the Turks, but I believed in my lucky star and that I could not die. He insisted so much that I finally climbed down, my pockets overflowing with daisies. I made a real feast of them.

It became impossible to go out during the day, even crawling, so we waited until after nightfall. We collected all types of plants without discrimination, but to tell the truth, not many were left. I recall seeing a dead donkey down on his side surrounded by much thicker grass; a stroke of luck! Eating – eating anything had become our sole obsession.

A boy named Abraham noticed a cat on a wall nursing her kittens. He told me, "Just grab her and I'll take care of the rest. I'll give you almost half of it." I darted out to catch the poor animal when the girls saw me and could easily guess my intentions. They started screaming and held onto my feet. Of course, the cat scampered away in a flash. The following day, I saw Abraham. He was eating meat and said, "It tastes exactly like rabbit." I was prowling around him to get his attention with no success. He did not even give me a bite to taste, claiming it was another cat he had found. Everywhere he could, he would write: "BREAD!

BREAD!" with a piece of charcoal. All the white walls were smeared with this distress call.

The director of the boys' orphanage, who was very irritated by these scribblings, warned us that he was seriously looking for the culprit. An exemplary punishment would be given. One morning, while we were in our dorms (which were also used as classrooms) waiting for our teacher to return, Abraham stood up and with splendid self-confidence walked to the closet, opened it, grabbed our teacher's lunch and swallowed it in a single gulp. Our teacher, an Assyrian lady who did not belong to the orphanage staff, had to bring her own food. She came in, saw the closet door wide open and screamed, "Who dared to open my closet and eat my lunch?" Abraham stood up and without shame admitted his theft, "I did it . . . I was starving!" For a moment, forgetting our misery and empty stomachs, we laughed at our friend's boldness who added with relevance, "If you'd been as hungry as we are, you wouldn't have left your meal unattended."

The director was informed and had no other choice but to punish Abraham. Other similar goings-on occurred quite frequently. I remember a boy who, once in a while, would pull a dry bone out of his pocket, lick it with delight and put it back in his pocket. Another one would only eat half a raisin at a time so we nicknamed him 'half-raisin!'

Other misconduct took place. Some orphans, organized in a small efficient team, had successfully opened the supply depot and had helped themselves generously. It lasted until the day they were caught and punished. At least, they did not suffer from hunger for a good while! Finding food was everyone's dream and worry. On the victory day, our first move would probably be to run to the first bakery, grab the bread, and eat it to the point of choking.

The orphanage also had its dead. In my class, the person in charge of chores asked for three volunteers to run a mission outside. I hesitated to raise my hand because of my weakness that day, and three of my friends, much quicker, took on the risk. One was shot through the heart, the other was seriously wounded, while the third one escaped and managed to come back unhurt. Another friend, who was standing a few steps away from me, had his foot up on a bench to tie his shoes and got shot in the hand by a stray bullet that came through the window. His name was Zaza, and he was from a Kurdish tribe of that name; he spoke a specific dialect.

Worse yet to come, we got infected by vermin. Starvation was one big struggle, and lice became another one. Days went by and we were filled with dread. We thought that if the Turks emerged victorious, the mass killings would be resumed.

XLI

On March 1, the first French airplane flew over the city. We all started to shout and believed it was a miracle. I had never seen a plane before and I cried out, "My God, my God! It's an eagle!" It was so high in the sky. The Turks were firing in its direction. Soon, the word spread that the plane had dropped a large package over the French forces with the promise for future reinforcements.

A sergeant and some French soldiers were staying in the orphanage and communicated with their headquarters by light signals. The French troops, approximately 500 men, expressed concern: the days were passing by and the promised substantial reinforcements never seemed to arrive – although they were stationed at Telabiat, not far from us. A rumor was circulating that the commanding officers were working out a compromise with the Turks. The troops could then withdraw and join the main body stationed at Telabiat.

On April 12, a friend climbed up on the sill of a condemned window that was overlooking a hill. We used all the cracks between the stones to inspect the surrounding area. He called me, "Come! Come quickly!" I thought he had seen some Turks moving forward in the trenches so we had to warn the guard on duty in our orphanage. But that was not it. I pulled myself next to him and I caught sight of a man coming down the hill waving a large white flag.

Indeed, the war was over and men – Turks and Armenians alike – were coming out of all the trenches and hiding places. The French forces had withdrawn the night before and the Armenians, left alone with the Turks, became frightened.

The following day, war clamors and roars of joy filled the city streets. In spite of the promise of mutual peace, the Turks had entrapped the French in the crossing of a valley named Chebeki. The French had all been slaughtered in the most abject bloodshed. The heads of the commander, as well as other soldiers, were carried in triumph around the streets, stuck on top of bayonets. The Turks, at the height of excitement, were singing their own "Marseillaise" and it was a dreadful one. Ours, the one we learned with so much faith and hope of a better future, was buried deep in our desperate hearts.

And France ignored the names of all her martyrs, again and again, as if nothing had happened.

I endorse what had been revealed in this case and I approve the severe judgement the French commanders of Telabiat received. The French military staff heading the strategic forces had not anticipated any back-up plans, including withdrawal or reinforcement.

Here are the facts:

The French troops of about 500 men arrived in Urfa to replace the British forces, with no artillery units and under weak leadership. As soon as they had settled, the unrest started and violent clashes took place at increasingly shorter intervals.

The Mouta-Saref, Ali Riza, Prefect of Urfa and ultra Kemalist, was staying in the city to secretly organize the entry of undercover armed forces.

The Armenians, who had felt the danger and the impending disaster, had requested weapons and ammunitions from the French. The demand had been declined. However, the Armenians managed in good time to round up numerous means of defense.

Ali Riza was engaged in double-dealing. On the one hand, he was advising the French to leave, granting them sufficient protection; on the other hand, he was providing the militia forces important strongholds in the city.

The five to six thousand Armenians, with their seven hundred orphans, had gathered in their own district. Thus, the city counted three types of forces.

On February 9, 1920, at nine in the morning, the Turks started shooting on the French and on the Armenian district, which fired back fiercely. The Turks falsely claimed that they had just wished to cross the Armenian district, with no intention of hurting any of them; they wanted to attack the French forces. The Armenians replied that the French had asked for the same favor and that, under these circumstances, would allow no one to pass. The Turks used their divide-and-conquer tactics but the Armenians maintained control over their district, acted wisely, and did not fall into the many traps set for them. The two-month long attack had been particularly harsh and the soldiers who had fought in the trenches suffered terribly.

The Armenians knew the Turks and the premises very well; they were helping and advising the French through Lieutenant Marserou and his twelve soldiers, who were stationed in the Armenian district. The latter used light signals to send the information collected by Armenians to the French forces.

This little war was not operating to the full satisfaction of the Armenians, who expected the French to openly attack the militia forces; they would have been easy to defeat if the Armenian tactics had been carried out.

The French refused all forms of direct conflict. The Armenians then established contacts with the Turks, concealing the fact that it was done at the request of the French. Some Armenian delegates introduced themselves to the Turks, saying they could act as intermediaries to negotiate a possible ceasefire with the French. The Turks, quite satisfied, gave their agreement.

It so happened that the Turks and the French met and thereby agreed that the French would withdraw. After two months of hostility, the French troops left Urfa. The departure took place on April 19 at midnight.

The Armenians showed them the route to follow, which avoided the mountains. It was longer than the usual one but they would be better protected from any ambush that could arise from the tricky gorges.

The commander refused to listen to this wise piece of advice. He had no reasonable grounds to question the word of the Turks, who would not dare betray an agreement that had been set under international military conventions.

At the last minute, when the tricolor of France was lowered, our one-hundred-year old Sarjou shot himself in the head, refusing to accept the terms of such a humiliating surrender. Lieutenant Marserou, who had lived with his dozen men in the Armenian district, sadly parted from several Armenians who had become his friends. While shaking their hands, he told them, "I am not saying farewell, but only goodbye, because I am sure we'll be back to take over Urfa."

The unfortunate man had no idea that the following day he would be dead.

The French troops, assisted by the Turkish mounted police, set out on the mountain road passing by Acaba on the way to Suruj. They were supposed to join the main body of the French forces in Telabiat.

The troops were crossing the valley of Shebeki when the mounted police disappeared suddenly. Then, a strategic ambush slaughtered the entire expedition.

Not a single man survived and some Armenians were among them.

At Urfa, the Armenians who had not left their trenches yet heard gunshots, which sounded like thunder coming from Acaba. They immediately realized that the French soldiers had fallen into a trap.

The following day, the Turks were celebrating their cowardly attack and victory with great jubilation.

Two days later, on April 12, a Turk came down the hill with the white flag, followed by Prefect Ali Riza and the commander of the militia forces. They were meeting the leaders of the Armenian defense with promises of peace and security between the two communities: the Armenians would be allowed to move around the city and get food supplies freely.

The Armenians, who were quite suspicious, asked the commander: "What guarantees do you propose? What is your offer so we can take your word for it?"

Commander Namek answered, "I know you have good reasons to doubt our word because it's a fact we always took advantage of our position. All I can say is you'll keep your weapons. What else do you want?"

Thus, the Armenians kept their weapons and, little by little, were free to move around. The Turks respected the agreement.

The situation lasted several months and the Armenians went back to their activities or businesses.

But disturbances recurred as the Turks showed signs of aggression and arrogance with arbitrary arrests and the murder of innocent Armenians. Events were taking a nasty turn. The Turks felt empowered and victorious following the withdrawal of Cilicia by the French.

Furthermore, according to what we heard, the French had broken the promise they had made to Armenians. They had signed an agreement with the Turks. The illustrious signatories were Henry Franklin-Bouillon, Léon Bourgeois, Georges Picot and many others.

At midnight on December 31 of the year 1921, the tricolor of France was definitively removed. With it and forever, Armenia under French protectorate, disappeared.

The French had not judged us worthy enough or deserving enough to be granted their support. In their eyes, we had less value than Djibouti.

Thousands of Armenian soldiers, called from around the world to help occupy Cilicia under the French protectorate, were demobilized to let the Turks replace them. The ones who had escaped from the slaughter, the survivors like me, were once more sent back into an endless ordeal.

More than five hundred soldiers died for Urfa; they have faded into oblivion up to this date. And two million slaughtered Armenians; do they matter?

If they have lost their Cilicia, their "wonderful Djibouti," who cares?

XLII

But let's return to the orphanage, right after the declaration of peace.

In the Armenian district, everyone was going to the center of town to get food supplies. The director of the orphanage allowed the ones with some money to go out and buy bread or treats. I only owned two *kurush*, which I had earned selling a pair of socks I had knitted. I had managed to get my raw material out of mattresses, by pulling handfuls of good wool here and there, which I had carefully hidden. During class, under my desk, I was secretly spinning my wool, my hands swiftly moving around a pencil. Later, I would knit the yarn with a wooden hook which I made. It took me several days to earn my two *kurush*, and I really deserved them. Finally, my turn came to be allowed to go downtown. There, in the first bakery I saw, I bought a piece of bread, which I eagerly devoured.

We soon returned to our tent village that had remained intact, except for some destruction due to the war. We met a dozen orphans on the premises, who may have stayed during the conflict to secure the place, and had suffered much less hardship or deprivation than us. Our new food rations were reduced even more: at lunch – our only daily meal – we were given a half-loaf of bread with a handful of raisins. I was always famished. After food distribution, it was trading time. Each orphan, according to his needs and tastes, swapped whatever he had. I usually offered my raisins against bread; a difficult deal to conclude, and even tougher when the raisins were replaced by green onions, as it sometimes happened.

We had too little food to eat and we were tortured by hunger. Many teenagers were leaving the orphanage and they were not held back. I decided to do the same. I would find a good master in town and then go. I told myself, I am old enough now; I can read and write; I am fluent in Armenian, as well as in Turkish and Kurdish; I can even speak some English.

I also had another good motive to be yearning freedom:

The director of the school had chosen me, among all my classmates, to recite a poem on New Year's Day. My part consisted of imitating the barking of a small dog. I had to bark;

then declare in English how much I loved my master; how faithful I was; and what a good guard dog I was. I had to punctuate each statement with proud barks: "Arf! Arf! Arf!" I was very displeased and refused to play the part. I was too ashamed to appear in that role in front of my friends. However, I could not avoid it. I had the best barks. I was the victim of my own success. I refused to be the hero of this ludicrous and absurd farce, and I set my mind to go.

Finally, the day came when I left the orphanage for good. I went to town. I wandered around and lingered outside the shops, in hopes of being noticed. Everyone, and Armenians in particular, could recognize the uniform I was wearing. However, I was not bold enough to ask for help. I just walked back and forth in front of an Armenian grocery store, which was the largest purveyor of food for the orphanage. My little trick finally paid off, and the owner called me in. Of course, he had guessed my intentions, being so obvious, and asked me if I was willing to work for him. I gladly accepted. He told me I had to inform the head director, Miss Holmes, about my intention to leave the orphanage. If she refused to let me go, I would have to run away.

I walked back lighthearted. I had never thought I could be hired so quickly. Was I finally in luck? At the orphanage, I met my friends and recounted my good fortune, but I soon realized how painful it would be to part from them. We had shared great sufferings, little joys, and a common fate, and we had forged strong brotherly ties between us. Nevertheless, it was my day – *my* lucky day. I ran to meet the head director so she could grant me the permission to leave.

I stood in front of the administrative building where her office was. I waited several hours, and she never came out once – nor did she even approach her window. I got tired of waiting and I returned to my tent. The following day, however, when the bell rang for breakfast, I quietly sneaked out and passed through the

Urfa street scene.

entrance gate of the orphanage forever. I ran to my new master. I explained to him that I had failed to get the permission to leave. I had fled. He told me it was fine.

I spent the rest of the day observing the work so I could make myself useful, as soon as possible. My master's partner was about to move elsewhere, and my help was needed fairly rapidly. By the evening, at the closing of the shop, we went home. After a fifteen-minute walk, we arrived in front of an old entrance door we pushed to reach a courtyard. It was surrounded by a one-story building with a rooftop terrace, where four to five families lived. I had already explained earlier that during the warmest time of the year, people slept on their roofs, according to local custom.

My master first introduced me to his wife, who was holding an infant in her arms, then to his sister, his brother, and his brother-in-law. They all lived together in the next room. Everybody stared at me and seemed satisfied. I myself was glad to at last be in an Armenian home where my native language was spoken. Besides, we had endured the same terrible suffering, which brought us even closer together. I was happy as I had never been for years, and my eyes filled up with tears. I lived as if I were in a family. Then, I remembered the very different receptions my Kurdish masters had given me, not so long ago. I had no master anymore; I had found a boss. That night, we shared a good meal, and later, they made room for me on the carpet so I could sleep.

The very next day, my boss bought me everything I needed. I exchanged my uniform, the one of the orphan and lost child, for street and working clothes. And, I wore a fez on my head. I became a man: I became what I wanted to be.

In a short time, I learned the trade and sales business. I would see Kurds passing by the store with their donkeys and I would happily yell, "*Lo apo wara, wara!*" (Come in! Come in!) I was in good spirits and joking with everyone. When my boss needed one or two load carriers, I would shout in Turkish in the middle of the marketplace, "*Hambal agha! Hambal agha!*" (Chief carrier! Chief carrier!) and the bystanders would laugh. A dozen persons would rush up at the same time, but only the first ones were kept. Carriers were always available in the city because of the shortage of work and extreme poverty. In the streets, many miserable beggars and abandoned, famished dogs would hang around, hoping to catch any type of litter thrown to them. A butcher's shop faced ours and dozens of dogs were always at the door, seated on their hind legs, waiting anxiously. Often, all at once, they would leap up to their feet; they knew every one of the butcher's actions and exactly when he would throw them some meat waste. It never touched the ground and was snapped in the air by the fastest dog. While working, the butcher held a swatter to ward off the flies buzzing around his meat.

I was getting used to my new life. Of course, the difference between the little shepherd – all alone on his mountain top with sheep and wolves – and the young worker, busy amidst a noisy crowd in an animated city, was huge. I was learning a lot of new things. Our Turkish neighbors asked my boss where he had found me. They would ask me if I knew a boy at the orphanage as smart and resourceful as I was. I would answer I did not know such a person; I did not want any of my friends to have the misfortune of working for a Turk.

The white-bearded *hodja* (village elder) living across the street promised me a *medjid* (Turkish currency) a day to stay in front of his shop and boast about his goods to attract the Kurds. It was an easy and well-paid job to do, but I would never return to work for a Turk, even if I was offered a fortune. Sometimes, I led carriers loaded with food supplies, all the way to the orphanage. I liked going with them to meet my friends and make an appointment to see them on the following Sunday, our common day off. I was bored without them; I did not know what to do or where to go. I was truly suffering from the separation. Still, I advised them not to leave the orphanage. I now knew the severe poverty of cities. Good jobs were scarce, and I thought of myself as privileged to have found one.

XLIII

In spite of my enviable situation, I felt terribly lonely. I missed my friends a great deal and I had to convince myself how fortunate I was. I had all I needed to eat, and I had gained weight – wasn't that the main thing? Other friends who had run away like me, did not get my lucky break and could not return to the orphanage. The rule was strict. We had to endure our freedom at whatever price it was.

One morning, while I was standing in front of the shop, I saw Ramo, my eighth master. I had kept sheep for him, and he was the one who, after my first escape, had declared I was not worth a single bullet. I approached him, raised my head to look at him, and said to his face in a loud voice, *"Merhabo, Ramo!"* (Hello, Ramo!). He stared at me with big curious eyes, wondering who I was and how I knew his name. Of course, some time had elapsed since then and I was not Azo any longer; I was a free teenager, well-shod, well-dressed, clean and plump. He stood there in front of me, stunned. I repeated, *"Merhabo, Ramo!"* He nodded his head trying to recall his memories. At the end, I finally added, "Don't you remember me? I am Azo." He then asked in a hushed voice, *"Lo, lo! Tu Azizi?* (So, you are Azo?) What are you doing here?" I showed him the shop where I was working. We talked a little, then he left to get his brother, the one who had found me hidden in the wheat field. Other village people came running. They had all traveled to Urfa to get food supplies. And here we were talking together as equals; there were no masters and no slaves anymore. Then, most of them left, except for one old Kurd I knew well. I stayed alone with him and asked him what had happened after my successful escape, and how long had they been looking for me? He gave an honest answer and besides, he had nothing to hide anymore. He said, "I was with them and we searched for you in all the neighboring villages. By chance, we learned you were in Avak so we went there. When we arrived, we found out that you had left the village just the week before. We gave up and stopped looking for you." I thought Providence had saved me – and that I had narrowly escaped the severe reprisals those barbarians would have inflicted upon me!

The word quickly spread that I was in Urfa and soon, those who came to the city did not miss the opportunity to pay me a visit. I told the story of my sister, who had been cowardly abducted before my eyes, to the Kurds who might provide me with some information. Some told me they had looked for her with no results; others said she had lost her mind. According to some farmers, she would have fled to the desert where she had probably perished. How could anyone not lose their mind when, under death threats, her brother and mother were forced to undress and were left naked? How could anyone not lose their mind when the abductor, after collecting their miserable rags, abandoned her sick mother and her young brother in the middle of nowhere? How could a virgin of eighteen not lose her mind when the disgusting and hated aggressor abused her like an animal? I could not soothe my heart from the terrible fate my sister had endured . . . from the martyrdom she had suffered, which was a much greater horror than death.

One day, Ibrahim Bekir's sister-in-law came to see me. She had been Mariam's boss. I had played with her children and in Mederbaz, I had fought with her son. He was still complaining about the cut on his face, which I had given him. His face was forever marked by an ugly scar. It probably had not been treated with appropriate care. She told me all her misfortunes. Her husband had been caught stealing a large number of sheep and had been shot dead. According to local custom, the family had received some type of reparation for the loss. However, the two brothers of the deceased had also claimed their shares. The orphans argued for their uncles' rights, seriously injured one, and put the other to death. The son who did the killing married his uncle's widow. Ibrahim Bekir was not involved in this tragedy and had remained neutral. I led my visitor up to Mariam's house and the two women met again with great joy. As poor as Mariam was, she was better off than her old mistress. She gave her some money and tobacco and then, they both kissed and bid farewell.

The following day, Ibrahim Bekir showed up at the shop to see me. It was his wife who had kicked me out, completely naked, calling me a dirty *giavour*. I also remembered how Guley, their little daughter, and I had gluttonously swallowed the yogurt prepared for the whole family. And here was Ibrahim Bekir, my old master, standing in front of the shop, miserable-looking and somehow intimidated. I had to take the first step and reach out with a smile to shake his hand. This, however, did not build up his confidence because, in his opinion, we belonged to different worlds: he had remained poor whereas I had become rich. He could only tell me, *"Lo djigki para ney medey du nomeymeney, bookhariet."* (Lo, give me some money; you ate my bread.) I was hurt by his words and I curtly retorted, *"Lo khera bavettey noneykharemet ez shooghoolan bekeremet."* (Lo, you did not feed me to honor my father. I worked for you.) However, I agreed to help him and to give him a *medjid* I had saved. But my boss interfered and told him, "He worked to earn his bread. He doesn't owe you anything." Several times I tried to hand him some money, but each time, my boss stepped in. I was very distressed because I could not assist him in any way. Was it Ibrahim Bekir's poverty, his oddness, his clumsiness, or his unfairness that displeased my boss? I did not know. He then left very disappointed, looking pitiful with his clothes in rags and his worn-out shoes. I watched him go for a long time, and the thought of not having been able to give him some money to relieve his poverty – for only a moment, makes me sad even today.

Thus, I saw everybody again: all the masters, mistresses, or fellows who had played a role in my captivity. I even saw Hamed Ali, the young Armenian I had kept sheep with and who had always refused to run away with me. Once again, I offered to take him to the orphanage, where he could probably find some relatives. He strongly objected. Did he still fear the idea of becoming a *giavour* again?

One has to count by thousands, the number of Armenian children who had become and remained Muslims, feeling terror or a strong repulsion for self-questioning. They had been so deeply brainwashed into believing the lowness of a *giavour*, that the slightest idea of returning to be one was too humiliating. Hence, they had lost their identities and their souls forever.

I now knew a lot of people, mainly my boss's friends, who would come to the shop for a visit. I was very busy and every day, I learned more and more about life.

Once in a while, two men dressed in military uniforms would come inside the shop. They had golden buttons on their jackets and carried a record book in their hands. They would check the goods, set the amount of taxes, and require immediate payment. I remembered that one day, as they stopped in front of our shop and asked for two *medjids*, my boss paid without any discussion. But elsewhere, it was not always the case. Long bargaining was involved between the taxpayers, mainly when they were Turks, and the tax collectors.

They would come to the shop three or four times per year to collect the different taxes. This was a convenient and speedy method used for the uneducated population, where only a few could read and where administrative hassle was inappropriate. Other government agents were charged with fraud repression. Inspectors would arrive, for example, at our neighbor the baker's; they would take several loaves of bread at random, and come to weigh them on our scales. Our weights were also subject to inspection.

The streets were noisy and animated. Little merchants with loud cries were constantly moving around, offering the passers-by all types of food or objects. Every morning, a man with a wicker basket on his head, loaded with loaves of bread, went by and shouted, "The marvel of the bazaar has arrived! Piping hot! Piping hot!" Several times a day, the coffee man walked by, serving burning hot coffee upon request, drunk in one gulp. He would mark a line in chalk for each mouthful taken, on the exterior wall of the shops. Regularly, he would sum up each customer's marks and be paid back the arrears.

The streets were also busy with an interminable coming and going of children. Each with a string around their neck, they hung a basket packed with things they could negotiate, such as matches, cigarette papers – tiny objects with no retail value. I carefully observed all those little merchants and paid a lot of attention to their activities, thinking I could eventually make a living if I lost my job.

XLIV

Time went by. One day, I found out from my friends that the orphanage would soon be tranferred to Lebanon. It was first a rumor that later became a reality. I wanted to leave with them. But, how to do so, since I was a runaway from the orphanage? I was somewhat bewildered and my anxiety was growing day and night. My boss noticed it and told me he would speak to the financial administrator of the orphanage when he came to the shop to buy food supplies.

This financial administrator, a man of Arab origin, was heavy and ponderous with a stern, closed face and only spoke when he had to. However, he promised he would present my case to the head director and ask for my reinstatement. When we saw him again, he declared that his request had been denied: no escapee would be readmitted. I would not return to the orphanage; I would not go with my friends. I cried out of anger and despair.

Around me, the political climate was deteriorating. Gradually, Armenians were leaving Turkey in secret. It was a fact that the Turkish government was issuing a limited number of passports and would only allow older women and children to depart freely.

I personally knew a lot of people. Near our shop, an Armenian called Krikor tended a small tobacco stall. He was a tall, strong, handsome man with a nice mustache. He was very popular. He often came over with other men and talked feverishly about the events occurring by the day. To the tired ones who wished to leave the country, Krikor retorted, "How do you dare think and talk like that? Are you forgetting we must avenge all our brothers? How can we abandon the tons of bones of our dead to the people who are our enemies? Have you lost your mind? Are you oblivious to their memory as martyrdom?" His face lit up with passion. He believed a miracle could happen. He never thought at any point that he would have to leave the country.

I liked this man for his enthusiasm and I decided to share my personal problems with him. I told him how a large number of orphans had already left. I wanted to join them. Krikor stared at me, saw my tears and the distress on my face. What could he expect from me? I was just a child. He promised to take care of me. Indeed, a couple of weeks later, he had settled my case. One evening, he discreetly led me to the coachman called Mouhla, a young Turk with a smiling face. He was married to an Armenian I knew from the orphanage, and he was a father. This woman's younger brother had already fled and she asked me to give him some family news if, by chance, I ever met him.

Mouhla told me that three Armenian women, who had received their passports, were due to leave in a week at the latest. He suggested I could join them and he would lead me to Jeraboulous at the Syrian border for 160 *kurush*. It was estimated to be a two-day trip. I informed my boss of this plan, who did not challenge the agreement we had concluded together. Unfortunately, my savings were no more than 80 *kurush*. My boss offered to pay the remainder. It was then agreed that I would give 60 *kurush* when we reached the border. My boss would confirm payment of the balance of 100 *kurush* to Mouhla in writing, after his return – if, of course, I had safely completed my journey.

A few days later, prior to the morning of my departure, Krikor left for Suruj to settle a personal case. This city, which I have already mentioned, was located halfway between Urfa and the Syrian border. At Suruj, he would wait for the carriage which I would be in, on its way across the city.

The coachman had instructed me to be prepared to leave very early the following Sunday. I was told to wait for him on the outskirts of the city, well beyond the checkpoint. When the time came and with great sadness, I bade farewell to everyone, as I would never see them again. My boss's brother, who knew the way, led me to the meeting place. Thus, together, we crossed the city in the early morning. Then, beyond one or two hills, we found a shelter, protecting us from the customs officers' control of access to and from the city of Urfa.

We silently waited for the arrival of the horsedrawn carriage. After quite some time, in the distance, we spotted two of them following each other. We thought that more passengers than anticipated were traveling. Then, the customs officers stopped the carriages. Finally, they resumed their course. When they came close enough, I recognized the one driven by Mouhla. I shook hands, said goodbye to my companion, and quickly stepped out of my hiding place. I climbed inside and the vehicle departed, and so began a new chapter of my life.

XLV

A little later, we were navigating a narrow pathway winding through a deeply nestled valley. Immense boulders were hanging on both sides. The coachman told us we were in the Valley of Chebeki, the very place where the French army had been slaughtered, as their trust had been betrayed. I opened my eyes wide and was filled with dread: every inch of this land had been washed out with human blood, and cries of distress had echoed in this solitude. My heart was heavy and my soul was sad. Mouhla remained silent, overwhelmed by sorrow. He was

Turkish but he could only feel repulsion and pity when remembering this shameful victory.

When we came out of the valley, he pulled himself together and asked me to sing "*Bardzir Aghpiur*" in Armenian. I did not know the words and offered to sing something else. He refused and, with a loud voice, he started the song with the first lines of the chorus. With the singing and chatting, we lost track of time and Sare Moughara soon appeared in front of us. There, everyone climbed down and Mouhla gave his horses food and drink. When we left, he asked me to go around the hill, in case of police controls.

I did what he said and walked beside the desolated hill. Suddenly, I realized I was not far from the place where I had kept my sheep. Memories came flooding back: I must have come through here with Cheko to go to Mesopotamia. And as I stared at the country of my slavery, my heart leapt for joy, because now, I was a free man.

I took one last look at these hills I had so longed to leave. My childhood dream was becoming true and was even exceeding my expectations, although it took quite a long time to get there.

On the other side of the hill, Mouhla signaled that I should climb aboard. Once again, we sat together, and our journey continued. He had not been inspected. However, Suruj was difficult to cross, and he was concerned for me, since I had no papers. And if I was arrested and turned back, he would lose the money I owed him. He was only paid in the event of a successful result. He told me (as well as reassuring himself), "Once we have passed Suruj, you will no longer be in danger of being discovered."

At sunset, the carriage entered the city of Suruj. I was concealed under a blanket with the women quietly seated on top of me. Upon request, I came out of my hiding place, all red and half-suffocated, realizing that we were in the middle of the courtyard of a large inn. I was directed to a stable, where I was to go and hide. It was dark and I waited for the arrival of Krikor for quite a long time. Finally, he made it there and noticed my state of anxiety and sadness. He held my hands. I gave him his brother's letter and he was pleased. He encouraged me by saying, "You are lucky I am in Suruj; checkpoints are very strict here." He then led me to an Armenian family, where I spent the night. The next day, I was taken back to the inn.

Everything was ready for the departure except for the last control checkpoint we were waiting for. Then, Krikor arrived with two police officers who asked for our passes. They had been informed of a runaway and they asked me if I knew about him. I answered I did not. After the control, the travelers climbed onto the carriage, one by one. I waited for my turn, standing anxiously by the footboard. Finally, the officers told me I could get on, after Krikor had successfully made arrangements. I thanked him by nodding my head and climbed next to Mouhla. We left.

I thought: The Armenians are getting slaughtered and the Turks don't even allow them to leave. How unfair! In fact, a large number of Armenians had to pay a high price to reach the border, disguised as Kurds, in carts loaded with goods. I could feel all the anguish and misery in this smuggling of human beings. However, freedom was not free and the methods used, after all, did not matter.

Finally, we reached the banks of the Euphrates River and Mouhla's job stopped there. He asked me to write the letter to my boss that would inform him of my safe arrival at the destination. I did it and gave him the 60 *kurush* I owed him. The remainder would be paid by my boss, as agreed.

A huge metal bridge crossing the river had been built by the Germans. But it had been blown up by the very ones who had made it – or their allies – in order to stop the advance of the Franco-British troops. It was impassable and another means to cross over had to be found. A young Kurd came up to us and offered to tell the French soldiers stationed on the opposite bank (meaning the Syrian territory) about our arrival, provided we pay him a small amount of money. We accepted the deal. He knew his job well and ventured forward the furthest way possible on the damaged bridge. He then screamed at the top of his lungs for someone to come and pick us up. Soon after, a large canoe, manned by soldiers, arrived and landed. Here we crossed the Euphrates River with hopes of entering a new world. Now, Armenians – very much alive – were carried over this large and indifferent river and were pushed by its current towards freedom.

XLVI

We disembarked and the soldiers led us towards the nearby train station. Travelers and refugees were waiting in a large room for the train to Aleppo, which came only once a week. It was expected in four to five days. It did not matter whether the wait was long or short; we were in the Middle East with a different concept of time, and we had already been waiting and waiting for so long. The following day, the last caravan of Urfa's orphans arrived and I immediately ran towards them to offer my help. They were so glad to see me and astonished, too, because I had preceded them. We shared our belongings and our worries, and during those few days, we renewed our ties of brotherhood, eating and sleeping together.

I was quite surprised when I recognized that the man who was leading this last group of orphans, and who was responsible for their arrival and food supplies, was the building administrator of the orphanage. He was an overweight, conceited person. Back in Urfa, my boss had tried to draw his attention to my case several times, but he had ignored his pleading. He did not seem fond of me. He recognized me, of course, but he granted me neither a word – despite all my smiles – nor a look which would have comforted me. He was completely indifferent to me, and I felt as if my presence was an inconvenience, too: I was an extra mouth to feed. However, I must admit, he never voiced the slightest criticism when I shared the meals with my friends. At last, one day, the train entered the station; it was the first time I had seen one. I was watching, genuinely amazed at this squat-shaped machine, spitting thick black smoke, wheezing, and breathing hard. Inside the locomotive, I noticed through the reddish glares of the fire, a man with a face quite blackened where only his white teeth and white eyes were gleaming. I had already seen railroad tracks on my way to Mesopotamia, when I had worked with my master Ramo, but I did not know what they were used for. Today, I knew.

Now, the orphans' luggage, mattresses and blankets needed to be loaded onto the train. With my friends' approval, I volunteered to do the job, taking advantage of the task to prepare a little secret spot where to hide, in case I would be denied the pass to travel freely.

The next day, we were asked to line up in formal rows. An American woman came to take a count of the children and reported the total number to the station officer with no comments, which was a good omen for me. When this was done, we climbed into the freight cars where we sat on the floor. The signal for the departure was soon given. We were in a state of wonder and at the height of excitement when we felt the train rattling and shaking under us. I was traveling to the big city of Aleppo, and I was with my peers, my people; it was perfect bliss.

Later, the convoy stopped and a train conductor entered the train car with a list of names in his hands. It was another control checkpoint and another moment of terror for me. When he walked up to me, he greeted, shook my hand and gleefully said: "Welcome among us!" He knew me well and I knew him; he was my boss's friend. He was a young, intelligent, and alert Arab who had left Urfa to return to his country. Of course, he did not report me and was delighted with the happy ending of my situation. I was no longer an illegal immigrant! That same day, at nightfall, we caught sight of the lights of Aleppo, and our hearts leapt for joy.

From Aleppo train station, we were led to a kind of inn near the Babel Faraj Square, where rooms had been prepared for us. I slept peacefully, relieved to be finally in good standing. However, early the next morning, Mr. Takavorian, the director of the orphanage for boys, who had already been on the premises for several weeks, came in carrying a large enrollment register. Another hurdle to overcome! When would all this be over? But, after staring at me with a twinkle in his eyes, he told me, "Well, you've really put on some weight at Hovanes' store! Yet, you are back!" I smiled shyly and he registered my name in the orphanage records. At last, my legitimacy was established: I was formally enrolled with the others in the book of the chosen ones.

XLVII

In Aleppo, where we stayed for four days, we did not get the chance to see any sights. Still, we realized what an old, busy, and picturesque city it was. We were back again on the train, heading towards Beirut.

In Beirut, and for the first time in my life, I saw the sea. I could not stop admiring it. It was magnificent! Later, we were transferred onto trucks to reach the orphanage of Ghazin, located on top of a hill overlooking the city. At night, from the balcony where I was sleeping (there was not enough room inside for all of us), I would contemplate with delight the city lights and the stars shimmering on the sea.

The following day, I was back with my friends from Urfa, who were mingling with the orphans from Marash; they spoke

Turkish amongst themselves. The girls' orphanage was situated a bit further. All my buddies were happy to have me with them again and the pleasure was mutual. There, I recognized the brother of the young Armenian woman, who was married to the Turkish coachman Mouhla. I gave him news of his sister and brother-in-law but he looked annoyed and refused to hear more. We had to undress and put on our new uniforms. I personally wanted to keep the clothes my boss had given me, as an act of loyalty and also by preference. But I could not breach the rule; I had to comply with it, in exchange for the security provided by the orphanage. It was only fair.

Afterwards, we were divided into different groups, based on our classes. I was glad to return to school, which I missed so much. I really enjoyed studying. Our Armenian teacher, whose name was Mr. Khahigian, came from Marash. His previous students had been very lucky; our teachers back in Urfa were not as talented. He would teach the Armenian grammar and history with contagious enthusiasm. We all loved him and called him "Dad": it was an affectionate nickname which he deserved well, since he was so fair and kind to each of us. Another one, Mr. Dekhrouni, our French teacher, was so intense and passionate in class that saliva would foam at the corners of his mouth.

Unfortunately, we were not able to take advantage of those dedicated teachers for long. Barely two months after we had settled, we were scattered into different buildings, newly constructed or about to be completed, so we could give room to the thousands of orphans evacuated from the different cities of Turkey, including Marash, Adana, Tarsus, Mersine, Kharpert, Urfa, Malatia, and more. Other large numbers of orphans had been already directed towards Greece or elsewhere. All the newly arriving orphans had to find a place in Beirut or its surroundings, such as Antelias, Jbeil, Nahr Ibrahim, Mamoulten, Ghazir, Aghazir. The older orphans were divided into two groups, one sent to Antelias, the other to Jbeil. Antelias, located near Beirut, was my destination, as fate had decided. There, we were mixed with other orphans coming from Adana and Tarsus, and then divided into classes, according to our level of knowledge.

The director of the Center, Hovanes Kouyoumdjian, was Armenian of course. He wore glasses, was constantly smiling, and showed great kindness to us. At the orphanage, we were well fed and the general atmosphere was relaxed, friendly, and safe. Some of the orphans, who had already received an Armenian education, were teaching us some sports, including swimming, which we practiced every day.

The director would join us in our traditional dances, and we would all dance together, with our arms and hands intertwined. The older students organized a band. The orphans from Urfa, amazed, were discovering the joy of living: *"la joie de vivre."* After a while, some of the oldest ones, who had been assigned a few initiatives, felt jealous of our director's popularity and created problems, which the main office in Beirut heard about. One day thereafter, assistant inspectors representing that office came over with new plans to improve the management of the orphanage.

Soon afterwards, our director announced that new orphans, more of our brothers and sisters, were on their way to join us. Except for the younger ones, we had to all go and work on a piece of land purchased for the construction of a large orphanage. A big factory used to be there, located by the seaside, just a few minutes' walk from our orphanage. Every day, in turn, each class would carry out a task. I was selected to join the first group, the one which had to start the clearing up. Armed with shovels and mattocks, we left for the worksite with our director. On the premises, we started our day of labor by saying the prayers our Lord had taught us, and our hearts filled up with courage. All over the place, small ponds of standing and smelly water could be found. Some said a silk mill had stood there, others a tannery.

The buildings with collapsed roofs were falling into ruin. It turned out to be a day of great removal of debris, as we all breathed and swallowed thick dust. At nightfall, worn out, we ended our first day of work far from realizing that that place would later become the Armenian diaspora's religious center.

The sad convoy of Kharpert's orphanage arrived some time later. There were girls – young girls dressed in rags – who had suffered food deprivation, poor hygiene, and exhaustion, and looked prematurely aged. I will never forget the sight of those emaciated figures. It would have reminded me of the horrors of the deportation – had it not been for the beaming smiles of newfound freedom radiating from the girls' faces!

XLVIII

I immediately ran to greet them and ask them where they were from, hoping to meet someone from Amasia – or at least find some clues that could lead me to someone from my hometown. I was holding on to the unreal dream that I would recognize either my sister or a relative in one of them. Alas, none of them came from Amasia, nor did the others, who arrived in caravans afterwards. There was every reason to believe I was the soul surviving member of my family.

Like the boys, the girls were placed at Ghazir and in other orphanages; we were all sent here or there at random, following the orders coming from Beirut.

As a result of a reorganization of the orphanage all the boys fit for work were called to leave for the annex, located some distance away from the train station, and where several hundred teenagers had already settled. Carrying our mattresses on our backs, we moved to the new residence, which was still under construction. While waiting for its completion, we lived like campers, eating outdoors and sleeping under the stars – with sometimes the surprise of the unexpected. Some of us would wake up in the morning, lying directly on the sand, our mattresses having disappeared during our sleep. The mystery was soon unraveled: under the moonlight, some vagrant children had crawled on the ground, moved stealthily between the rows, pushed the sleepers softly onto a bed of sand, pulled the mattresses, and ran away with them.

The days were not much of a comfort to those troubled nights. We had to work under harsh conditions, and we were so badly fed: only a rough loaf of bread with some olives. Sometimes we were served a rice soup where a large number of fat worms were floating. It was disgusting but we had no choice; it was our only menu. I was so hungry that I would gobble up my share and my mate's as well, he being unable to eat out of revulsion. Orphans who were dissatisfied were allowed to leave. No one was kept by force. The orphanage was saving us from starving to death and we owed our benefactors a debt of gratitude.

A new administration staff then took over. The new director, Mr. Nelson, was American and would stutter a little, as I remember. He was trying his best to run the orphanage, which was a very difficult task due to the lack of cohesion between the orphans: they came from different provinces, were affected by multiple influences, and had endured diverse horrifying experiences – which had a strong impact on their personalities. The orphans themselves had a hard time blending together as a single group. In my opinion, the best ones were from Kharpert. They behaved with integrity, showed more discipline, and lived the values of the Gospel, for they had received an in-depth religious education. I rapidly became friends with them and often attended their Bible meetings, where my faith was strengthened by God's word.

During our daily field work, we kept busy repairing large wooden barracks, each of which could hold three to four hundred people. The big refectory was the only building constructed of strong material. My job, along with several others, was to carry bulky sandbags on my back, from the beach to the buildings, over a distance of about one hundred meters.

The supply of labor was plentiful since the orphanage had more than a thousand boys. After a few weeks of organization, the workload was divided as follows: work in the mornings and studies in the afternoons. However, even during my period of hard labor, I did not waste my time at all. I put my small book of English stories in my pocket and at each rest stop I managed to memorize two or three words. I would repeat them in my head until the next work session. Slowly but surely, I built up vocabulary while carrying sandbags.

XLIX

Some of my friends who stayed in Jbeil lived under better conditions, were properly fed, and never took part in the construction of the orphanage. It was my fate to be sent to Antelias and I needed to be patient.

New teachers arrived. Mr. Boujikanian, who was our principal, ruled the school like a large family and coped with the difficult situation as best as he could. The quarrels and the fights were recurrent and misunderstandings usually turned into a general conflict. The strife reminded me of my seventh master Ramo's camels: like them, we arrived from all directions and had not grazed on the same grass.

To lessen the rivalries, our teacher wrote a song – even better than that, an anthem! Every day, we would sing along together and slowly our fights, although they did not stop, became increasingly scarcer.

Here are the lyrics of this soothing song:

"We are brought here from many places,

And we now form a large family,

Our home is Antelias, lovely Antelias,

Our beloved school Antelias,

Here, there is no longer Kharpert or Gesaria,

Neither Marash, nor Adana, Tarsus nor Talas,

But our beloved and beautiful Antelias.

Long live our benefactors,

Hurray to Australia,

Let's go forward and keep marching,

Let the straight roads shake under our feet,

Let's march with our hands by our sides,

Our steps echoing as we go forward."

Australia is mentioned here because it partially took care of us; maybe it was to unburden the Near East Relief foundation?

Sometimes, teachers would argue among themselves and challenge the head teacher about ideology. The latter, who was a person of faith, used to teach us The Bible and several religious songs. Thus, the extremist patriots rebelled against him. Mr. Aghazarian, in particular, would angrily declare, "You take the children away from their nation. You are hurting our country."

After six months, the construction of the three large dormitories was completed. At night, we slept in them and during the day, we studied there. We were therefore well-protected against the weather – but alas, not against the bedbugs swarming all around. We found a practical trick to protect ourselves at night: we had sewn together our sheets into sleeping bag sheets, and only the tip of our noses would stick out, allowing us to breathe!

Even with my bad nights, I would wake up at dawn and go to the beach with my books. Sometimes, I was so early I had to wait for the light; I would then read my lesson facing the sea, in the coolness of the morning. I was aware of how much I had fallen

Antelias, studying at the orphanage.

behind in my studies, compared with my friends. During the year I had spent at the grocery store, I had gained weight and confidence, but I had not attended a single class. I was not the only one to leave the dorm at dawn. Almost every morning, several of us would sit on the sand and await daylight.

I soon took an exam and the results were so satisfactory that I was allowed to skip two levels. I was admitted to the first class. I had caught up with my friends and made up for the time lost outside the orphanage. However, out of the forty students, I ranked last. Most of my friends spoke English fluently and some spoke French, of which I did not know a word; it was all new to me.

One day, a very sad one, the teacher told me I did not qualify for the class any longer. I became deeply distressed and humiliated. I intensified my efforts, studied harder, and was desperately eager to succeed. One morning, as we were coming back from our break, the teacher gave us an arithmetical problem to solve. All the students bowed their heads and started writing. I held mine up straight because I had not understood the facts of the problem. I dared to ask the teacher to read the text over for me alone. He agreed, reminding me once more, I was not in the right grade level. After this second reading, however, everything became clear to me: it was the very subject I had just studied during recess. I solved the problem quite easily and was the first one to submit a solution – which seemed correct to me – to the teacher. He was so convinced of my mediocrity and failure, he first refused to even look at my slate. However, he did look at it after a while. My answer was right, and I had been so quick that obviously all cheating was excluded. Indeed, with the exception of four or five students, the others did not pass the test, since the problem was such a difficult one.

From that day on, I stopped being the dunce of the class. Others replaced me in that very unpleasant position. I had proved my determination; I had gained our teacher's confidence, and thus, managed to stay in the first-level class. I was happy and proud. As I stood in the rows when the first class was called upon to advance, I could not help looking behind me and watching all the tall boys who remained. I had passed them with success: I – who was so little!

L

It was around this time that I received a letter for the first time in my entire life. It was sent from Jbeil. There, in Jbeil, I had a cousin! Of course, I promply wrote back. Fortunately, we had the same name, since our fathers were related; otherwise, we would never have been reunited. Some of my friends from Ghazir, who were sent to Jbeil, put the two names together – and that was how the incredible miracle happened.

One day, he came to visit. We hugged and held each other tightly. We could not hold back our tears of joy, even though we had just met. He told me his sister was alive and staying at Ghazir. With the orphanage's official permission, I went to see her one morning. It turned out to be a sad meeting. I did not recognize her and I had nothing to give her. Despite all the terrible events we had experienced – in fact, precisely because of that – we said very little. We looked at each other almost like strangers, not understanding why we were orphans. She allowed me to write to her and as tenuous as this relationship was, I did not want to lose it. We kept exchanging letters.

Another day, shortly afterwards, I met a young teenager in Antelias who claimed to be from Amasia. His mother, who had escaped the pogrom, was living in Beirut. I begged him to write to her and ask if she had any news of my family. Was one of them still alive? A few days later, he came back carrying a message for me, including an address where I could go. I obtained another permission and left for Beirut to visit this place. There, I had the great joy of recognizing friends who, in Amasia, used to live in the same district as my family. They were brother and sister, and I recalled playing with their younger brother when I was a child. They took me around to visit other neighbors from my hometown, especially a woman who had known my family well. She was so glad to see me. And she gave me the good news: she recalled seeing my sister Mariam – the one who had stayed at Shar Kishla – at the orphanage of Marsovan, near Amasia! This lady was certain my sister was alive. I spent my day in a wonderful feeling of friendship with the illusion of being home. I returned to Antelias confused, restless – but so excited.

All that cheerful news, however, took me back into my horrible past, and I felt quite agitated. From then on, I gave myself one goal . . . one thought: to find my sister. She had been lost and she was about to be found again. We both had the same parents, the same blood. I dreamed of living with her. The idea of reuniting with my sister became an obsession.

LI

A few weeks later, the director announced that all those who wished to work in France were summoned to register at his office. Many of us replied to the proposal, and I was one of them. I was hoping everything would become possible on the other side of the Mediterranean – even meeting one of my relatives.

However, I could not help but regret withdrawing from school. I was learning so well now, I loved studying, and I had so much more to learn. Did I really have to give up my classes to go to France? What would happen to my education over there? I was facing so many unanswered questions, I could not stop worrying. But France . . . how impressive! I successfully passed all the health tests and was declared "fit for France."

I was about to leave Antelias; the Antelias I thought I would never like. Now, I wished I did not have to go. I knew from experience what it meant to quit the orphanage. I had made a commitment to myself never to go away, unless it was required. However, today, I was breaking my own promise . . . but how could I pass up such an opportunity? I reflected upon it for an entire week, carefully weighing the pros and cons. At the orphanage, we ate very little indeed, but we were one team, drawn together by extreme misery, and strengthened by our faith in God.

At this crucial point in my life, ready to sail towards an unknown but hopeful destination, I fervently thanked God for having saved me from death on so many occasions. I also thanked all the members of Near East Relief who helped me start a new life. Their names included: President Dodge H. Cleveland, Henry Morgenthau, James L. Barton, Samuel T. Dutton,

Alexander J. Hemphill, Harold A. Hatch, Stanley White, William W. Peet, Edwin M. Bulkley and Charlie V. Vickrey. I finally thanked all those who, at some point, had helped us and all the thousands of anonymous benefactors who made it possible for us to survive. Now, with their support and generosity, we had become young men and women, able to work, and in turn, assist our neighbors in need.

It was in Antelias where I providentially found my cousin and heard that my sister was alive. It was also in Antelias where I learned how to serve and worship God; where I pledged to love my neighbors in His name, in all one love. So often, on that beach with my friends, our faces turned towards the sea, we had prayed and adored our heavenly Father. With all my heart, I gave thanks to God who had protected me from hardship and helped me find again the true Faith, especially here in Antelias, whose memory I would forever cherish. May all glory, praise and thanks be given to our Lord in this home by humble children like me. Many of the words spoken and heard here made my faith grow and led me into Christian life.

Finally, the day to bid farewell to the orphanage had arrived. I had been looking forward to this departure with mixed feelings of joy and great apprehension. On November 5, 1923, we boarded the magnificent all-white French liner called *Canada*. She would take us across the sea to the shores of an educated, Christian, and humanitarian country – the country of freedom and human rights.

EPILOGUE

My father disembarked in Marseille and was soon sent to work in the Gers, on an isolated farm in the Southwest of France. There, people did not speak French together; they spoke a local dialect (*patois*). My father's dream of a formal education was never fulfilled. He kept running away from the backward farms where he was placed by the French government, always eager to find a better and more educated environment.

One day, he received a letter from his cousin – who had the same last name – informing him that his sister was alive and well in the United States. Papken and Mariam continued writing over a period of almost thirty years, unable to embrace each other because of the American immigration quota. In 1955, they finally reunited in New York City, after forty years of separation. By then, my father had moved from Bordeaux to Paris, was married and the father of three children. Little Papken outlived most – if not all – of his fellow group of refugees who survived the atrocities of the Armenian Genocide. He died at the amazing age of 104 and is now buried in one of the most famous cemeteries of Paris, *Le Cimetière du Montparnasse*.

In writing his memoir, my father had no literary ambition. It is the transcription of "The Odyssey of an Orphan During the Great Genocide," a book my father wrote in Armenian and self-published in Paris in 1951. His first notes were taken aboard the ship *Canada* as he headed for France – and were fresh from his childhood memory.

When he retired, he decided to have his personal testimony translated into French under his strict supervision. His story was then adapted into a book published by Garniers Frères (Paris) in 1980, under the title of *La Solitude des Massacres*. His deportation as a child, as recounted in these publications, was cited in 1984, in the work of the *Tribunal Permanent des Peuples,* held at the Sorbonne in 1984, at which he was chosen as one of the four personal witnesses of the Armenian Genocide. In addition, his story was recently selected and retold in 2011, by historian Anouche Kunth in the book *Les Arméniens en France,* published by Les Editions de l'Attribut. Now, I have translated his original document into English, in accordance with his deepest wishes.

Papken reunited with his sister Mariam, New York
City, 1955.

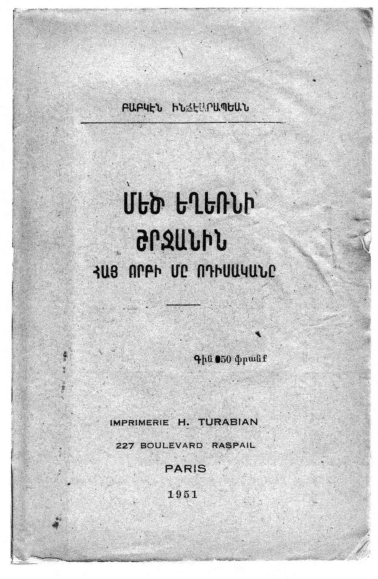

Papken Injarabian's memoir in Armenian, 1951.

Papken Injarabian, aged 96.

Also from the Gomidas Institute

ԿԻ

Child Memoirs of the Armenian Genocide

Jean V. Gureghian, *My Father's Destiny: the Golgotha of Armenia Minor,* transl. from French by Diran Meghreblian and with a preface by Yves Ternon, London: Gomidas Institute, 2015, 178 pp. pb., ISBN 978-1-909382-15-2

Avedis Albert Abrahamian, *Avedis' Story: An Armenian Boy's Journey,* edited with an introduction by Carolann Najarian, London: Gomidas Institute, 2014, x + 112 pp. pb., ISBN 978-1-909382-13-8.

Levon Shahoian, *On the Banks of the Tigris* (Youth edition), transl. from Armenian by Garabet K. Moumdjian, London: Gomidas Institute, 2014, 148 pp., map, illustration, pb., ISBN 978-1-909382-09-1

Vahram Dadrian, *To the Desert,* transl. from Armenian by Agop J. Hachikyan, London: Gomidas Institute, 2006, xviii + 410 pp., foldout map, illustration, pb., ISBN 978-1-903656-68-6

For the full range of our publications please visit our website at *www.gomidas.org*

CPSIA information can be obtained
at www.ICGtesting.com
Printed in the USA
BVOW08s0730010917

493485BV00001B/4/P